25 SKI TOURS IN THE WHITE MOUNTAINS

Flume Covered Bridge—a favorite with winter travelers (see Tour 17).

25 SKI TOURS IN THE WHITE MOUNTAINS

SALLY AND DANIEL FORD

 New Hampshire Publishing Company   Somersworth

Library of Congress Catalog Card Number 77-78189
International Standard Book Number 0-912274-75-1

© 1977 by Sally and Daniel Ford
All rights reserved

Printed in the United States of America

Photographs by the authors
Designed by David Ford

The book is dedicated to Katharine Serena Ford

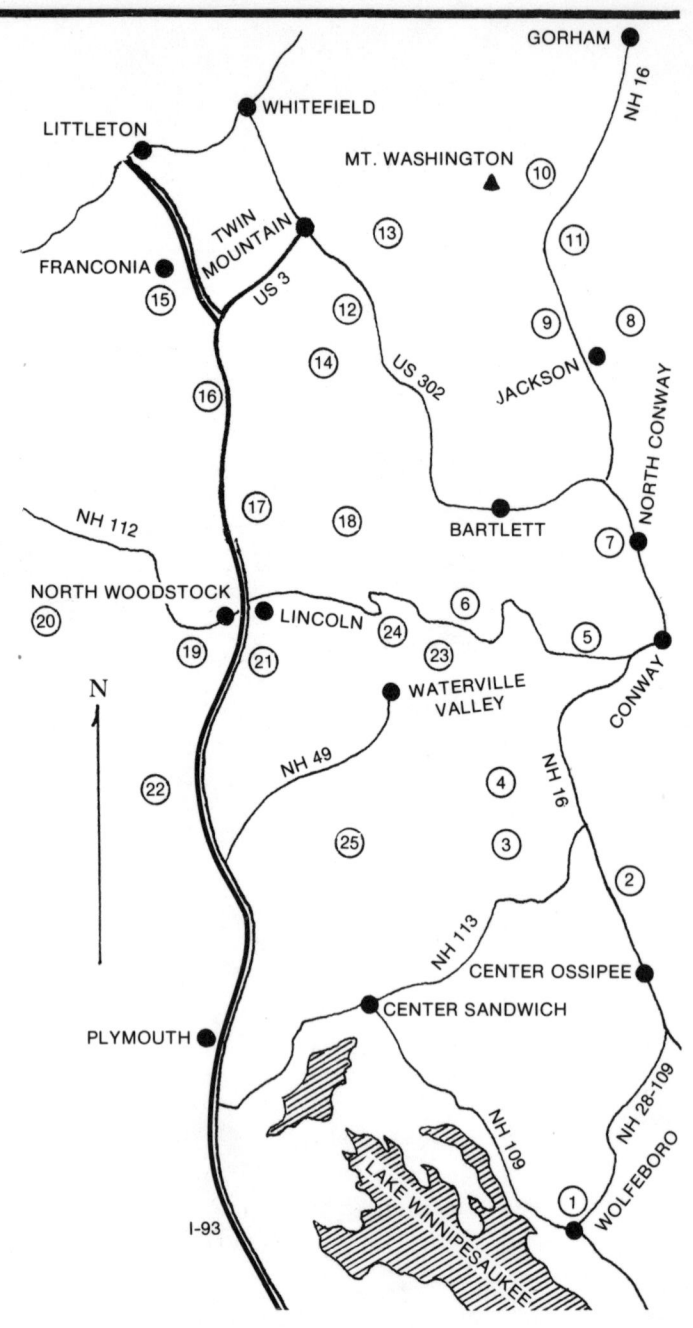

Contents

	Introduction	9
1	Abenaki Loop	13
2	Trout Pond	17
3	Hemenway State Forest	22
4	Paugus Brook	27
5	Deer Brook Loop	31
6	Rob Brook Road	35
7	Diana's Baths	40
8	Black Mountain Loop	44
9	Ellis River Trail	48
10	Lowe's Bald Spot	53
11	Wildcat Valley Run	59
12	Mount Willard	64
13	Ammonoosuc Loop	68
14	Zealand Falls Hut	72
15	The Inns of Franconia	76
16	The Old Man	80
17	Flume Gorge	84
18	Wilderness Trail	88
19	Peeling	92
20	Tunnel Brook	96
21	Russell Pond	100
22	Peaked Hill Pond	104
23	Avalanche Camp	108
24	Greeley Ponds	112
25	Sandwich Notch Road	117
	Tips	121

An invitation to the reader:

If you find that your favorite trail has not been included, or that a trailhead has been moved or landmarks changed, please write:

Editor, 25 Ski Tours
New Hampshire Publishing Company
P.O. Box 70
Somersworth, New Hampshire 03878

Introduction

Every book was written for someone in particular. "25 Ski Tours" was written for you, because you want to try your cross-country skis on something more challenging than the back pasture or the city park. We commend you to the White Mountains of New Hampshire. Without qualification, we recommend the White Mountains as the best and most beautiful ski-touring region between the Rockies and the Alps.

To be sure, you'd require a high order of ability to make a winter traverse of the Pemigewasset Wilderness or to ski above timberline in the Northern Presidentials. But there are dozens of White Mountain tours that can be accomplished by anyone with skis, a light pack, and an average constitution. We have chosen 25—among the foothills to the north of Winnipesaukee, through valleys and intervals, and along fair paths to the heart of the White Mountain National Forest. That's enough, in all likelihood, to keep you occupied for several years, especially since many of these tours give access to a whole network of possible skiing trails.

These tours are meant to represent the widest possible range of White Mountain experience. We have given you farmsteads, waterfalls, ghost towns, logging roads and railroad beds, lookout towers, wilderness shelters, and beaver dams. And ponds, of course—lots of ponds, which as places to *go to* just can't be equaled.

We favored trails that led to something of scenic or his-

Introduction

toric interest. We favored wide trails over narrow ones, and we favored trails that seemed likely to remain pretty much unchanged for several years. We tried to stay away from commercial touring centers, but this wasn't always possible—sometimes a touring center had the local monopoly on fine skiing. We also stayed away from beginner trails, although a robust beginner could certainly handle many of the tours in this book.

Inevitably, we found ourselves skiing some of the trails that veteran tour-skiers have been following for years. Other things being equal, we favored the new over the old, but too slavish a devotion to the principle would have meant omitting some of the nicest trails in the White Mountains. So we included a few of the classic routes, figuring that the veterans will forgive us while the newcomers will thank us.

* * *

For each tour, we list certain basic facts at the outset. The **distance** comes first and in most cases is measured from your parking space to your destination and back again—or around the loop, if it is a loop. A very few tours are "end-to-end" trails where arrangements must be made for return transportation, in which case only the one-way skiing distance is given (the Wildcat Valley Run, for example). We suggest that you begin with one of the shorter tours. Five miles is about right for all but hardened skiers or those who follow a rigorous and ski-oriented exercise program. In theory, you can always turn back if a trail proves too long, but in practice there is something compelling about a destination you have set for yourself. Save the long tours for later in the season, when your legs will be stronger and you'll have a few more hours of daylight at your disposal.

Introduction

Second, we rate the tour according to the **difficulty** we experienced in skiing it—slight, moderate, or considerable—after making allowance for the conditions prevailing that day. This isn't a perfect system, but should prove more consistent than the traditional scale of "novice," "intermediate," and "expert." We've never been sure just where we belonged on that scale. More important, these categories tend to break down whenever there's a change in the weather. With light powder to either side, a novice can handle some rather difficult trails; on ice or breakable crust, it doesn't take much of a slope to unnerve even an expert. So we have simply rated one tour against another, using ourselves as the standard of reference and trying to imagine what the skiing would be like under "average" conditions. Distance, incidentally, was not a factor in deciding whether a trail was easy or difficult to ski.

Third, we name the best available **map**—generally one of the Appalachian Mountain Club sheets—for the region in which you'll find yourself. (If you don't already own these maps, see Tip 18 at the back of the book.) A contour map is indispensable for backcountry skiing. Not only will it help you regain the trail if you go astray, but such a map enables you to travel the backcountry with more sympathy and understanding, as if you were both moving across the snow and soaring high above it.

A sketch map accompanies each tour. With a few exceptions, these maps are intended only as an aid in charting your route on the appropriate contour sheet. We have followed the usual conventions—north is at the top, buildings are represented by black squares, summits by black triangles, and so on—plus a few conventions of our own. The basic route is shown by a heavy broken line. Side-trails and side-roads are shown by dotted

Introduction

lines; sometimes they are skiable, but more often they are not. Stars are used to indicate points of interest.

*   *   *

We have not attempted to estimate the time you should allot to each tour. Skiers vary too much in the speed with which they'll cover a given trail; and the same skier, on the same trail, may find that yesterday's time must be doubled to allow for today's snow conditions. Then too, there is a vast difference between December and March in the White Mountains of New Hampshire. Early in the season, the shadows are long by two o'clock in the afternoon, and by three the glory has left the day. On a blustery January day, there is no such thing as an afternoon tour. Start in the morning and carry a picnic lunch; you'll double both your pleasure and your margin of safety.

Such variables cannot be neatly laid out, as in those charts which show the "chill factor" for a given temperature and wind velocity. They are matters for the skier's trail sense. "Trail sense" is not a mystical quality but a habit of making good decisions—about the condition of the snow and the state of the weather, about the strength of your party and the equipment you are carrying. When we skied the trails that make up this book, we tried to notice such decisions as they arose. We refined them as we went along, and then we assembled them in the form of "25 Tips" which you will find at the back of the book. Read them before you set out, for they will help you achieve the main object of ski touring, which is to enjoy . . . enjoy!

1 Abenaki Loop

Around the loop: 3 miles

Difficulty: moderate

Map: USGS Wolfeboro

Wolfeboro calls itself "the oldest summer resort in America," but the residents manage to keep themselves busy in the winter, too. The Abenaki Ski Area has been serving the town since the 1940s. In addition to the alpine slope and a jumping hill, the area now has a fascinating cross-country loop located on private land and maintained by volunteer labor. Visitors are welcome, providing they follow the local courtesies (no litter, no dogs, and yield the right of way to racers in training). The trail is a perfect introduction to backcountry touring, for it never strays far from civilization.

A sketch map, rental equipment, and other assistance are available at the Nordic Skier shop on North Main Street. From there it's a 3-mile drive to Abenaki Ski Area: turn right on Mill Street just beyond the ski shop, and follow that and Bay Street to its junction with Pine Hill Road—also known as NH 109A. Turn left and you'll reach the ski area in about 2 miles. If there's a chain across the entrance, you will still find room to park without blocking the access road.

The trail starts to the right of the warming hut, as you ap-

1   Abenaki Loop

proach it from the highway. For 100 yards it follows a tote road uphill and past the Abenaki ski jump; then an arrow directs you into the woods. The trail forks almost immediately. We turned right onto the Moody Trail, and following the loop in that direction does seem to make pathfinding a bit easier. (Trails are named for the farmers whose land they cross, and their names are subject to change each time you go through a fence.) The first ½ mile is a pleasant meander through what a real estate agent would call "growing timber"—i.e., scrub. Use care on the downhill pitches, because the trail seldom provides a runout before turning again.

The trail doubles back on itself and skirts a gravel pit before leaving the woods. Up to this point it has been marked with red tape, but now you simply ski across an open field with the highway on your right, passing fairly close to a house and barn. Soon another farmstead comes into sight ahead; it fronts on the Waumbeck Road, which obliges you to turn left for a few hundred yards be-

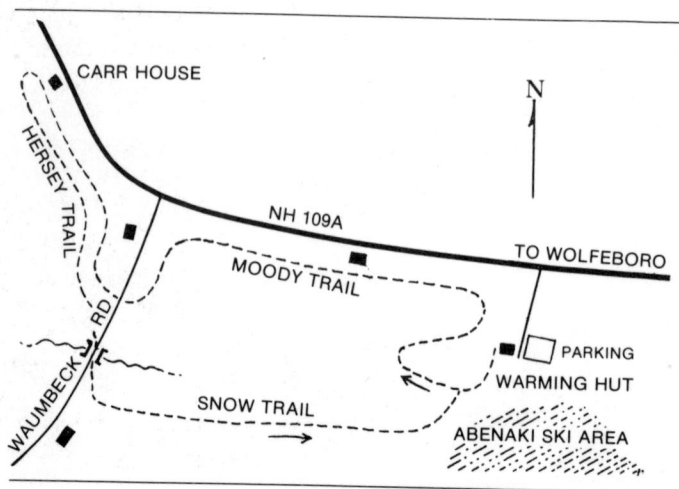

1 Abenaki Loop

The Abenaki Loop takes you close to the highway and the farmsteads that border it.

1   Abenaki Loop

fore reaching the well-marked road crossing. You are now on the Hersey Trail—several trails, in all likelihood. Ski back toward the state highway, keeping the farm a polite distance on your right. Turn left at the top of the hill and follow the highway as you did before. The trail goes through a stone wall, passes behind the Carr farm (built about 1810), and ends in a cul-de-sac. Either here or at the stone wall, you can find a sheltered spot for a picnic lunch, being sure to return all the remnants to your pack. All along this ridge there are splendid views of the Belknap Mountains to the southwest and perhaps the snowy peak of Mount Cardigan to the west.

After returning to the bottom of the Hersey field, you'll find that the trail—now marked with yellow tape—enters the woods straight ahead. It soon turns sharply toward the Waumbeck Road, then turns again just before reaching it. You skirt the road on the right side for a short distance, cross over at a brook, and skirt the left side of the road until yet another farmstead comes into view. Here the Snow Trail turns to the left. Although straighter than the Moody Trail, it passes through the same kind of woodland and follows the same tricky rule of providing a turn at the bottom of each little dip. It leads in ½ mile to the trail junction and tote road where you began the tour. You may find that the tote road is steeper on the descent than it appeared when you were climbing up, and that it offers a fine opportunity to improve your skill at snowplowing and pole-dragging.

When the Abenaki rope tow is in operation—afternoons, weekends, and holiday weeks, snow permitting—cross-country skiers are requested to sign in at the warming hut, and of course to sign out upon their return. Since the trails are not patrolled, this is the management's only way to know that everyone has returned safely.

2 Trout Pond

To pond and return: 5 miles (10 miles possible)

Difficulty: moderate

Map: AMC Chocorua-Waterville

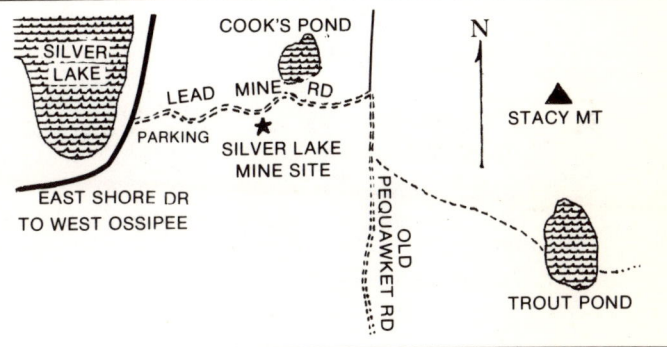

At the close of the nineteenth century, scores of New England towns were left to die as their young people joined the great migration to the westward. Their only monuments are cellar holes, stone walls, and the woods-road that was once a busy highway. Such a road can be found on the flank of Stacy Mountain, in Madison township. It can be skied for miles or used as a link in a rewarding tour to Trout Pond, on a hardwood ridge in Freedom. The latter was the route we followed.

Driving north on NH 16, turn right in West Ossipee at a blinking yellow light, just beyond the Mount Whittier

2 Trout Pond

Trout Pond is a natural picnic spot—sheltered from the wind, open to the sun.

2 Trout Pond

gondola. This is NH 41. Follow it east for 2¼ miles to East Shore Drive, turn right, and drive just over 1 mile to Silver Lake. Watch for an unplowed road on your right, with parking for one or two cars and probably with signs of snowmobile activity. This is Lead Mine Road, though no sign identified it when we went through. The first leg is an easy, winding, uphill route through a growing forest of hardwoods and evergreens—an excellent place to test your knowledge of the pine-tree family. By the end of the morning, we'd seen red pine (long needles in clusters of two), pitch pine (clusters of three), and of course white pine (clusters of five).

At the height-of-land, and just before the road turns downhill and to the left, the old Silver Lake Mine can be seen in the woods on the right. The mine is filled with water—frozen now and covered with snow—so it looks little more impressive than a gravel pit. (It's also posted against trespass.) After skiing downhill, you'll see Cook's Pond on your left, with the concrete remnants of the building in which the lead ore was crushed.

A bit more than 1 mile from the start, you'll ski uphill to a crossroads, plowed to the left, unplowed to the right. Turn south on the unplowed road, which is starting to fill in with scrub but which hikers and snowmobilers have kept open as a wide, straight path through the trees. According to the USGS Ossipee Lake sheet, this was once known as the Old Pequawket Road; town maps of the nineteenth century show it dotted with farmsteads, all of which have grown to forest again. Follow the road for perhaps ⅓ mile, until it dips to take you across a small brook. The side-trail to Trout Pond leaves sharp left amid a cluster of gray birch and white pine. It is not marked in any way but is wide enough to be a woods-road in its

Trout Pond

own right, and there'll probably be a snowmobile track to follow.

Ski southeast about 1 mile through a young hardwood forest, mostly uphill. The going is sometimes fairly steep, but eventually the trail levels off and you'll spot the rounded outline of Stacy Mountain through the trees on your left. Then the trail drops down to the shore of Trout Pond—large enough, in our part of New Hampshire, to qualify as a lake. It's a lonely, lovely spot for a picnic, with the gentle humps of Stacy and Blazo mountains the only landmarks in view. We're not sure about Blazo, but Stacy was the name of a farming clan in Madison township. The family graveyard is on the other side of the mountain.

On the return, control your speed as you descend from Trout Pond. The trail, as veteran tour-skiers like to say, is a bit "sporty" in places. You can easily pick up speed enough to raise your hackles on the turns.

If the day is still young, you can ski south on the Old Pequawket Road. You won't meet pavement until you strike the Ossipee Lake Road, 3 miles away. For the venturesome, a circle trip is also possible. The trail continues on the west shore of Trout Pond, meeting a north-south road in ¾ mile. A strong party could ski down to the plowed Ossipee Lake Road, skirt the pavement for about 1 mile, then come north again on the Old Pequawket Road. Consult the AMC and USGS sheets for this route, which involves a day's journey of about 10 miles.

3

Hemenway State Forest

To tower and
return: 4 miles

Difficulty:
mostly slight

Map: AMC
Chocorua-
Waterville

Tamworth is the very model of a New Hampshire village. Tucked between the Sandwich Range to the north and the Ossipees to the south, it's not on the road to anywhere in particular, so it remains almost untouched by tourism. So much the better for those who make the detour.

In the old days, Tamworth's "summer visitors" included Grover Cleveland, William James, and a certain Augustus Hemenway. While not as famous as some of his neighbors, Mr. Hemenway left a more enduring mark upon the landscape: he acquired several farms, totaling 2,000 acres and including the crest of Great Hill, and bequeathed them to the state of New Hampshire. Today this fine tract of land is known as Hemenway State Forest. It contains a lookout tower, a Scout camp, and boundless opportunities for skiing.

Tamworth is reached on NH 113. At the village center, drive north on NH 113A—also known as the Chinook Trail, in honor of a dog who trained here for an expedition to the South Pole. Look for a sign reading "Big Pines Natural Area." Hemenway Road is on your left, 1 mile beyond the sign (4 miles from Tamworth village). If you

3 Hemenway State Forest

miss the turn, take the next left and you'll arrive at the same destination, at the end of the plowed road 1/10 mile from NH 113A. There is ample room for parking.

The ski route lies to the south, following power lines all the way. Thus it's an excellent tour for those who are uncertain about their pathfinding abilities. We met no one, but we saw tracks aplenty—deer, snowshoe hare, snowshoe people, cross-country skiers, and of course that strangest of all winter travelers, the snowmobiler. The snowmobilers in Tamworth are mostly local, and they tend to stay in the same track instead of mashing everything in view, so the machine-packed trail was more of a help than a nuisance.

Hemenway Road is gentle to begin with, climbing through a mixed forest that must date back to the donor's time. (We measured one fine hemlock at 30 inches in

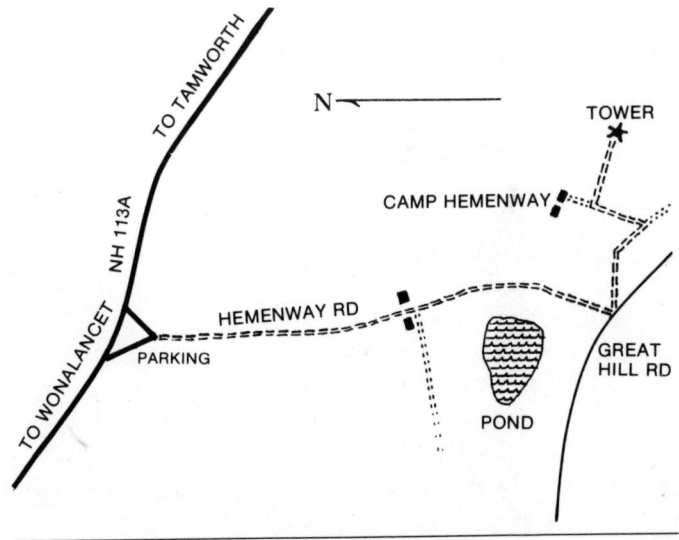

3 Hemenway State Forest

3 Hemenway State Forest

Dominated by Chocorua's snowy peak, the mountains form a mighty barrier to the north.

3 Hemenway State Forest

diameter, which in this climate is not far from maximum growth.) By the 1-mile point, the going is considerably steeper. Do not despair, for you have almost reached the height-of-land—and the return trip will be free! Soon the road begins to lead downhill, past a house trailer on the left and a cabin-garage on the right. Also on the right is a logging road which goes nearly 1 mile into the woods (see the USGS Mount Chocorua sheet). Then there's a steeper drop, a nameless pond is visible through the trees, and you find yourself climbing the last 100 yards to Great Hill Road, which is kept open during the winter. Sharp left, however, an unplowed road leads into the woods, with power lines running along it and a sign pointing to Camp Hemenway. Ski uphill for about 1/4 mile on this road. After the power lines enter the woods, and just as the road levels off, turn left for the Scout camp.

When the first building of Camp Hemenway is in sight, turn right and follow the power lines up to the Great Hill lookout tower, now closed for the winter. The access road is steep—side-step if you must, but do not fail to visit the tower. You can climb to the third level (exercising great care if the steps are icy) and discover that the grandest views in the White Mountains are not necessarily found north of Conway. Chocorua is the first to take your eye—a perfect alpine peak. The northern rampart is completed by Paugus, Passaconaway, and Whiteface. Southward lie the Ossipees and the white blanket of Ossipee Lake. You can see two villages as well, each marked by a church steeple: Wonalancet to the northwest and Tamworth to the southeast. Seeing them from this perspective, one feels great admiration for the men and women who came through the wilderness to build these settlements in 1766. If the land is so awesome today, what must it have been like two centuries ago?

4 Paugus Brook

Upstream and back: 4–8 miles, as you like

Difficulty: moderate

Map: AMC Chocorua-Waterville

Here's a tour for those who like to explore the backcountry at their own pace and without a given destination. The Paugus Brook valley narrows to the northward, with Mount Paugus on the west and mighty Chocorua on the east; the woods are mostly open, and with the brook running down the middle, it's almost impossible to go astray.

As for the previous tour, drive north from Tamworth on NH 113A. Not quite 3 miles from the village, turn right (northeast) on Fowler's Mill Road. The sign is inconspicuous, but you can recognize the turn by the fact that this is the second right since Tamworth and the first to lead downhill. Follow the road 1/2 mile past a bridge to a side-road on the left. This is Paugus Mill Road, and for a signpost it has the names of the trails that branch off from it.

It leads in a few hundred yards to a small green house, before which it makes a left turn. You'd be well advised to scout ahead on foot, for the continuation may not have been plowed clean. If it has, you can drive for about 1/3 mile to a turnaround; otherwise you must use your resources (and probably a shovel) to find a parking place.

4   Paugus Brook

Wherever you alight, follow Paugus Mill Road into the woods, where it is marked by orange blazes on the trees. They will lead you in short order to the summer parking lot. Here the Liberty Trail leaves on the right for Mount Chocorua. Go straight ahead on the Brook Trail, until it too swings off to the right. (Liberty Trail was once a toll road; Brook Trail was cut by the local people so they could climb Chocorua without paying tribute.) Bear left at this junction onto the Bolles Trail, which follows Paugus Brook to its beginnings in the Paugus-Chocorua divide.

Frank Bolles was a poet, naturalist, and secretary of Harvard University. One of his poems could serve as the motto of every wilderness traveler:

> Learn to tread the leaves with fox feet
> Like the hare to cross the snow-drifts

In 1891 he blazed the trail that now bears his name, following an old logging road from Tamworth to Albany. It

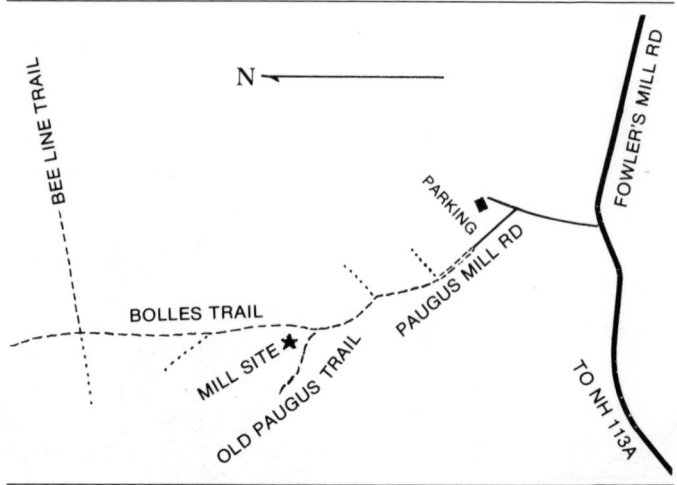

Not many years ago, Paugus Brook was clamorous with logging activity all winter long.

4 Paugus Brook

climbs gently through the hemlock woods on the east bank of Paugus Brook, then crosses to the west bank. All the crossings were bridged when we went this way.

Less than 1/2 mile from the first crossing, the Old Paugus Trail leaves on the left. This area is worth exploring, for it is the site of Paugus Mill, where the virgin oak of Tamworth and Albany was transformed into the pilings that support East Boston, in land claimed from Boston Harbor. When the trees were brought down from Mount Paugus, the final pitch was so steep that a teamster could see the backs of his horses from his precarious height above them. The load was "snubbed down" by steel cables—a business so thrilling that the townspeople used to snowshoe out to enjoy it. Now all that remains of this enterprise is a gigantic sawdust pile.

Beyond the mill clearing, the Old Paugus Trail slabs the south side of the mountain and can be skied for part of its length. Or you can continue north on the Bolles Trail, entering a region of young hardwoods. The route is not blazed in this area, but even a neophyte pathfinder should be able to follow the trail without difficulty. The Bee Line Cut-off soon jogs to the left; the Bolles Trail almost immediately crosses to the east bank of Paugus Brook, requiring two bridges for the task, one for a tributary and one for the main stream.

The final intersection is with the Bee Line Trail, connecting the Paugus and Chocorua summits. The western leg is not recommended, but you can ski north for more than 1 mile on the Bolles Trail or east about the same distance on the Bee Line Trail toward Mount Chocorua. When you're ready to return, you'll be surprised to discover that you have gained sufficient altitude to coast much of the way back to Paugus Mill Road.

5 Deer Brook Loop

Around the loop: 4½ miles

Difficulty: moderate

Map: AMC Chocorua-Waterville

We'd never explored Deer Brook, which spills into Swift River between two tourist attractions, a waterfall and a covered bridge. We asked the district ranger if he knew of any hidden ski tours along the Kancamagus Highway. As it happened, he'd just finished blazing the Deer Brook loop for skiers, using an abandoned hiking trail and a just-built logging road.

Drive west on the Kancamagus Highway (NH 112), whose entrance is south of Conway off NH 16. In a bit more than 6 miles you'll see a small parking area on your right, giving access to the Albany Covered Bridge. There's room here for several cars. If the snow is compacted—and it probably will be, for the bridge is popular with snowshoers and snowmobilers—you might as well carry your skis across. As you pass through the bridge, notice the trusswork which supports it. The basic truss is a multiple kingpost, but reinforced in this case by a huge laminated arch—a combination peculiar to the Conway area, where several generations of the Paddleford family devoted themselves to building such bridges. (For more about covered bridges, see Tour 17.) We sometimes think that the White Mountain National Forest is too good for its visitors: the arches, posts, and

5 Deer Brook Loop

braces have all been autographed with knives and aerosol paints.

Once through the bridge, turn left (northwest) on the unplowed Deer Brook Road, which follows Swift River. At this writing, neither the road nor Deer Brook Trail are shown on the AMC map; you might want to draw them in, using our sketch map as a guide. The road extends for about ¾ mile. Just before it ends, a rough logging road comes in from the left. This is your return route, and in early or late winter you should check it out to see if Deer Brook is passable. If not, you'll have to ski both ways on the trail.

The trail begins at the end of Deer Brook Road. The trailhead will probably be marked by the time you come this way, but in any event you can scarcely go wrong. There's not much room between the brook on your left and the rising ground on your right; if you lose the path, just bushwhack laterally for 100 feet or so and you should find it again. The climb is steady but not terribly steep—about 700 feet in the course of 1½ miles. In a few places you'll be clinging to the slope, and toward the end you'll actually be skiing up the brookbed. (The summer hiking trail crosses to the left bank but is impracticable for skiers.) Soon after, you'll see the logging road high on the opposite bank, and in a few hundred yards more you'll be scrambling up to a log "landing" the size of a suburban front lawn. Here the timber was loaded onto trucks when this area was thinned out. It's a fine picnic spot, or if you're adventurous you can ski up the logging road toward Moat Mountain. The Forest Service plans to use this road as a link in a ski trail that will end at Diana's Baths (see Tour 7).

5 Deer Brook Loop

The return leg follows the logging road downstream. There are two bridges which might be tricky: snow accumulates on the running surface but not on the crosspieces, making for an extremely narrow track. Between the bridges there is a 40-acre clearcut which offers a magnificent view of the southern mountains, from Mount Blue (Chocorua is hiding behind it) over to Passaconaway. Clearcutting is a forest-management tool which encourages "desirable" trees—white and yellow birch, in this case—to gain a foothold in an area otherwise dominated by less valuable species. Which goes to show that the National Forest, as the signs proclaim, is a "land of many uses."

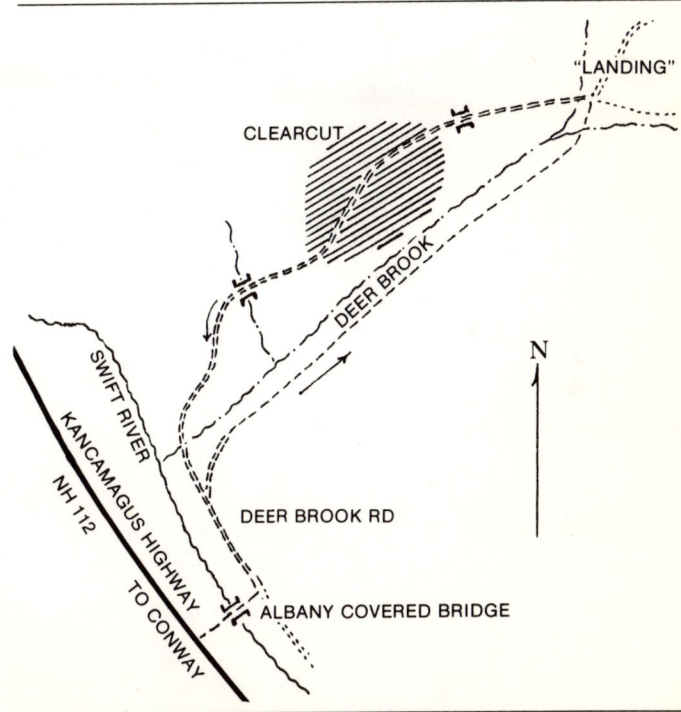

5 Deer Brook Loop

The final bridge, crossing Deer Brook itself, was scheduled for removal when the timber operation was completed. However, the stream is passable on skis except at times of high water. Once across, ski 100 yards to Deer Brook Road, down which you'll return to the Albany Covered Bridge.

Albany Covered Bridge provides a dramatic beginning to the Deer Brook Road.

6 Rob Brook Road

To bridge and return:
5¼ miles

Difficulty: slight

Map: AMC Chocorua-Waterville

The Kancamagus Highway has been judged one of the country's five most beautiful summer drives. In winter it's positively awesome. Following old logging railroads for the most part, it was completed as an east-west highway in 1959, paved a few years later, and opened for winter traffic even more recently. Now it's identified on the road maps by the mundane label of NH 112, Conway to Lincoln. Don't be fooled. It's a wild and lonely road when the snow is drifting on the wind, and in a severe storm you may find it closed altogether.

The eastern section of the highway follows Swift River through the Albany Intervale, once a hardscrabble community of farmers and woodcutters. About 12 miles from Conway, the Bear Notch Road leaves on the north; turn here and drive through an enclave of summer camps, oddly situated in the heart of the National Forest. (They were here before the Forest Service arrived.) About 1 mile from the Kancamagus Highway, you'll come to an unplowed road on the left. In recent years this road has been maintained as a snowmobile corridor, but there are plans to route the machines away from it, for it leads through one of the larger deer yards in the mountains. If you'd like to see how the whitetail deer pass their time in the winter, this is the place to visit. There is room to park

6 Rob Brook Road

on the west side of Bear Notch Road. The ski route can be identified by a gate and probably by snowmobile tracks; the first leg is downhill to a bridge over Douglas Brook. Then you climb briskly uphill and to the left—the only climb of any consequence you'll encounter today.

About ½ mile from the start, there's a splendid vista on your left, at what is obviously a turn-out for summer traffic. To the south is the ponderous bulk of Mount Passaconaway, with little Mount Hedgehog closer at hand. Southwest, the far ridge is dominated by the peaks of Mount Tripyramid, and in the middle distance is Mount Potash. The Kancamagus Highway lies between these mountains and your vantage point, but cannot be seen. (Passaconaway led an Indian alliance during the first white settlement of New Hampshire. He almost certainly could have thrown the colonists into the sea, but preferred to keep the peace by giving them the seacoast

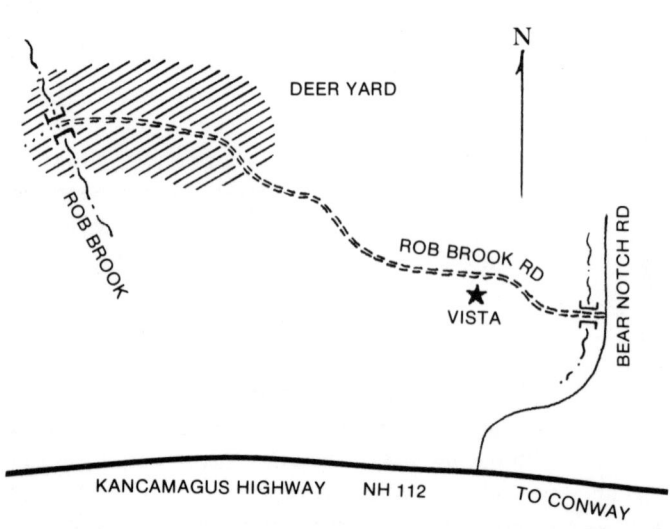

6 Rob Brook Road

In a hard winter, the whitetail deer must plow their own trails through the snow.

lands. His grandson, Kancamagus, led an attack upon Dover in 1689, but by that time the Europeans were too strongly entrenched for an Indian victory. By 1700, the alliance was broken and Passaconaway's tribe gone from New Hampshire.)

There are other outlooks along the way, and an occasional glimpse of mountains to the northwest, but none so grand as those you have just seen. Henceforth, the attraction is literally underfoot. About 1½ miles from the start, the road enters the Rob Brook Deer Yard. You should soon see tracks in the snow—trenches, they may

Weighted with snow, these branches seem to beckon the skier into a brand-new country.

be. Whitetail deer are rather small creatures and must wade through the snow if it is at all deep. For this reason, they are not native to the White Mountains: they couldn't outrun the cougar in the winter and did not move this far north until the big cats were trapped out of existence. Sometimes the deer will exploit a packed snowmobile track for a short distance before plunging into the woods on the other side of the road. Their droppings look like rabbit pellets and aren't very much larger.

6   Rob Brook Road

About 2 miles from the start, there's a signboard to inform you that you are leaving the town of Albany and entering the town of Bartlett. About 100 yards beyond, another sign explains that you have left Bartlett and re-entered Albany. Don't worry: you are still moving forward, and after a short downhill ski you will reach the end of the access road. Here there is a narrow bridge over Rob Brook, a clearing, and a hemlock grove eminently suited for a picnic. The Brunel Trail goes off to the south and could be explored by the venturesome. Others will be content to return the way they came and perhaps to explore one of the several logging roads that branch off to left and right.

7 Diana's Baths

To cascade and
return: 1 mile
(4 miles possible)

Difficulty: slight

Map: AMC Mt.
Washington

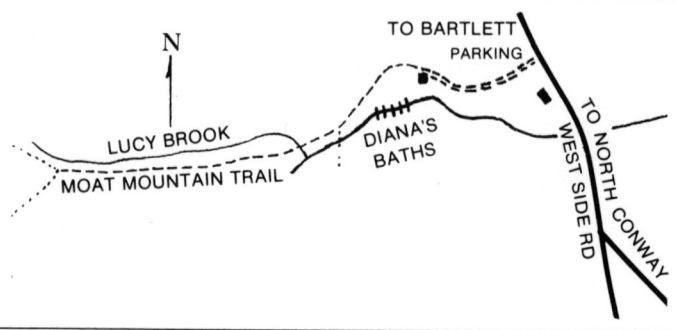

A century ago, North Conway was already hosting visitors to the White Mountains. Travel was a very serious affair in those days, when a stagecoach was the only public conveyance between the Conways and the outside world. Once there, the visitor was likely to remain for a week or two. The hotels kept their guests entertained by carriage rides to the local attractions, not the least of which was the cascade named in honor of Diana, the Roman goddess of childbirth and the forest. This is how one visitor described the sight:

"Still farther on we came upon a fine cascade falling down a long, irregular staircase of broken rock. One of these steps extends, a solid mass of granite, more than a

7 Diana's Baths

hundred feet across the bed of the stream, and is twenty feet high. Unless the brook is full, it is not a single sheet we see, but twenty, fifty crystal streams . . . falling into basins they have hollowed out. It is these curious, circular stone cavities, out of which the freshest and cleanest water constantly pours, that give to the cascade the name of Diana's Baths. The water never dashes itself noisily down, but slips, like oil, from the rocks, with a pleasant, purling sound no single word of our language will correctly describe."

What was a delightful carriage ride in 1880 is a delightful ski tour today. Driving north through the village, turn left (west) on River Road just beyond the Eastern Mountain Sports store. Upon crossing the Saco this becomes the West Side Road to Bartlett—covering much the same territory as US 302, but instead of motels and shops you are treated to the sight of farmsteads that have changed very little in a generation. One of these is the Lucy Farm, on the left, 2.2 miles from North Conway. It consists of a white house, gray barns, and a most remarkable silo with a dormer window at the top.

Look for a plowed parking space 100 yards beyond the farmstead, with room for four or five cars. The right-of-way to the National Forest leads due west across the field and is marked by parallel lines of electric fence. Upon entering the woods, you will find a yellow chain across the right-of-way. No snowmobiles or other vehicles are allowed past this point, for the Forest Service has designated Diana's Baths as a Restricted Use Area to protect it from overuse. Camping and campfires are likewise prohibited under the RUA designation. About ¼ mile from the highway, you will come upon a clearing and a boarded-up building which once served as a restaurant and inn. The carriage road ends here, and there

7 Diana's Baths

is a signboard to mark the beginning of Moat Mountain Trail.

Lucy Brook is in view on your left. The lower part of the cascade can be explored on skis, but use *extreme caution*. The same whirlpool action which carved the basins out of granite also has the power to undermine the ice—we found several basins open and purling on a cold day in January. A better plan is to return to Moat Mountain Trail and use it to gain access to the upper part of the cascade. There are occasional views northeast toward Bartlett Mountain and Kearsarge North, also known as Mount Pequawket.

Moat Mountain Trail is an old logging road, fairly wide, with no sharp turns, and nowhere steep enough to make skiing difficult. After lunch you will certainly want to explore it. About ½ mile from Diana's Baths there is a fork, with Red Ridge Trail departing on your left (not shown on the AMC map). Moat Mountain Trail goes straight ahead on the north bank of Lucy Brook. The brook soon turns, however, and you can follow the south bank for about 1 mile. Then you come to another fork, with Attitash Trail leaving on the right and the main trail turning left and beginning its climb to North Moat Mountain. At this writing, the trail was not skiable beyond this junction, although the Forest Service had plans to improve it as a ski route to the Kancamagus Highway.

The return trip to Diana's Baths is a lovely run, especially when the snow is fresh and you can control your speed simply by skiing off the beaten track.

◄ A sturdy snowplow is necessary when the trail slopes downhill. Soft snow makes it easier.

8 Black Mountain Loop

Around the loop: 7½ miles

Difficulty: considerable

Map: Jackson Ski Touring

For the most part, we dedicate this book to the proposition that the best things in life are free. Here we depart from that pleasant rule. The town of Jackson has transformed itself—at no small labor and expense—into the ski-touring capital of the Northeast. In return for maintaining 75 miles of trails, it asked us to take out a guest membership in the Jackson Ski Touring Club. Furthermore, we paid for this tour in the form of a climb so hearty that it made us long for ski-mountaineering equipment. But the tour was worth it—not only the $2 fee but also the sweat we expended on the uphill sections.

Jackson is the town reached through a covered bridge, off NH 16 as it begins its climb to Pinkham Notch. The Ski Touring Center is on your left as you enter the village; pay the trail fee here and purchase a trail map ($1), because your route is not shown on summer hiking maps. Then drive straight through the village on NH 16B, following signs for Whitney's Inn and Black Mountain ski area. When you reach this venerable resort, 16B becomes the Dundee Road, and there is a sign to this effect. Take your next left and drive ½ mile to the pavement's end, with parking for a dozen cars. This is the Black Mountain Road, though it wasn't signed when we passed through.

Black Mountain Loop

Ski straight ahead on the unplowed road, which immediately assumes the posture it will maintain for more than 2 miles: uphill. You'll pass a ski route on your left (Sugarbush Trail, circling back to Whitney's) and the Bald Land Trail on your right. The latter is your return route. We skied the loop in a clockwise direction and recommend the same to all but expert skiers.

The Black Mountain Road has now become the East Pasture Trail (#15 according to the local marking system). It skirts a meadow with a fine view of the Doublehead mountains to the southeast; then it begins to climb in earnest, topping out at the 2,500-foot contour behind one of the seven summits of Black Mountain. Here there's a junction. Turn right on the Woodland Trail (#52), which almost immediately rewards you with a gorgeous overlook upon the East Branch country. The valley's eastern wall is formed by Baldface, Sable, and Chandler

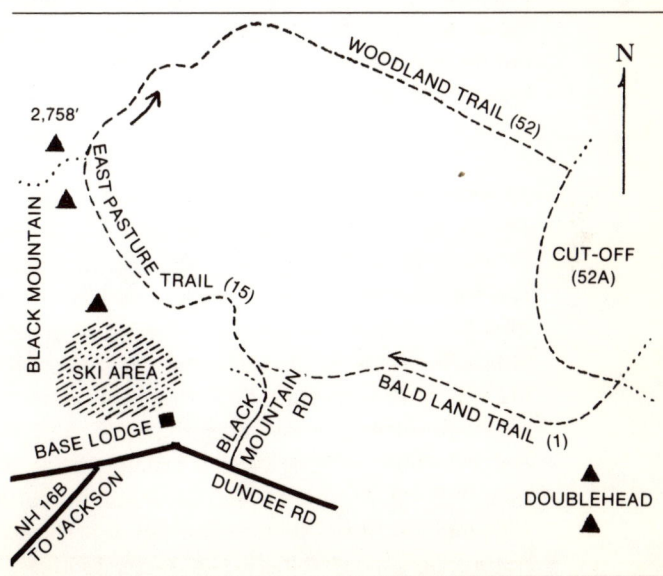

mountains. The AMC Carter-Mahoosuc sheet is useful for identifying the more distant landmarks, which are not shown on the Jackson ski-touring map.

After two tricky descents, the Woodland Trail leaves the evergreen forest and enters a region of new growth, which it traverses on an old road. For the next 2 miles you can enjoy some of the finest backcountry touring in the White Mountains.

About 4½ miles from the start, the trail again divides, with the Woodland Trail heading deeper into the East Branch country, and a cut-off (#52A) turning you toward home. The cut-off also follows an old road, until it ends 1 mile later at yet another junction. Here you must turn sharp right—uphill again—on the Bald Land Trail (#1). As you climb to the height-of-land, you are regaining 400 of the vertical feet you recently descended in such pleasant style. For the day, and discounting the minor ups and downs, you will have climbed and skied 1,300 vertical feet—nothing for an alpinist, but quite respectable on cross-country skis.

The Bald Land Trail takes you back to your starting place in about 2¼ miles, through the col separating Black Mountain from North Doublehead.

Like most of the Jackson trails, this loop receives considerable use—we met three parties on a weekday, something that rarely happened on our other tours. The track is therefore quite fast. This is a blessing on the level sections, a mixed blessing on the uphill, and a holy terror on the descent. Not for nothing does a downhill skier have the right-of-way! On a packed surface there is little you can do to control your speed. The remedy is not to pick up speed in the first place or to take this tour the day after a storm.

Old logging roads make for fast touring and distant views—Baldface Mountain in this case. ▶

9 Ellis River Trail

To inn and
return: 11 miles

Difficulty:
mostly slight

Map: Jackson
Ski Touring

This is everyone's favorite trail, and we've heard stories of a 250-skier headcount on holiday afternoons. There are two reasons for the crowds. First, people have the notion that the Ellis River Trail is suitable for beginners, which is nonsense. The minimum skiing distance is 5 miles, and there are plenty of sudden dips, so it's hardly the place to learn the joys of touring.

But even if the Ellis River Trail were posted for intermediates, it would still attract scores of travelers. It offers a near-perfect track, close by the water's edge, through hardwoods and evergreens and abandoned orchards, with glimpses of the alpine world above timberline, and a fine old inn at the end of the trail. If solitude is your pleasure, well, just leave at dawn on a weekday, and you'll probably have the whole lovely tour to yourself.

The most convenient parking is at the touring center in Jackson village (see previous tour). Ski west across the field behind the center, toward an eminence that is Green Hill; cross the Ellis River and NH 16. There's a bridge over the former and a tunnel beneath the latter, but neither looked very inviting when we made the cross-

9 Ellis River Trail

ing. In any event, ski along Green Hill Road (also known as Iron Mountain Road) until you're abreast of the second house on your right—the driveway of which is the start of the Ellis River Trail. (For those too lazy to ski this first ½ mile, parking may be possible at a wide spot in the road, just before the trailhead. Heaven help you, though, if you block this gentleman's driveway.)

Having found the trail, you'll require no more directions. The Ellis River Trail is the width of a jeep road for the most part, and there's a double track almost all the way. It's okay to ski side-by-side on a quiet day, but at other times the polite thing to do is keep to the right.

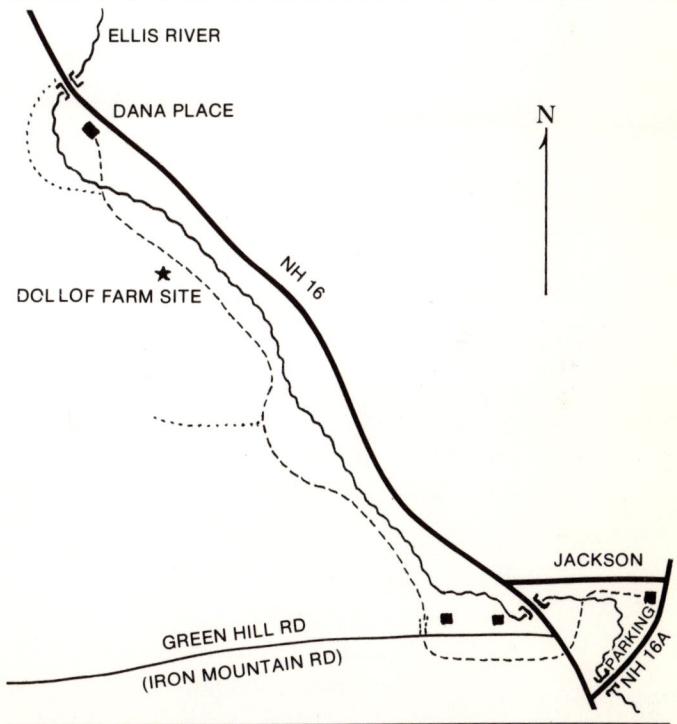

Ellis River Trail

The occasional tricky sections take the form of a quick climb and a quicker drop, and are all in the first half of the trip. They'd pose no difficulty except for the fastness of the track and the likelihood that another skier may be racing toward the same turn from the opposite direction. There are mileage markers at regular intervals—short miles, in our estimation. About 2 miles south of the Dana Place, you'll encounter a first-aid cache in a mailbox, and immediately thereafter a side-trail to Winnewetta Falls. This excursion is longer and more difficult than the map would suggest. About 1 mile beyond, there's a more feasible side-trail to the old Dollof farm. The summit of Wildcat Mountain is just visible to the north, and soon you'll see the majestic eastern slope of Mount Washington.

The Ellis River runs between you and the Dana Place. Normally the ice is safe, but at high water you must use the trolley which has been provided for your convenience and excitement. If you don't like carnival rides, you'll have to ski ½ mile around to the highway bridge, then walk back to the inn on NH 16.

A strong party can run the Ellis River Trail in an hour or two (the track record is 31 minutes and 48 seconds), so a half-day outing is feasible even if you plan to ski both ways. One-way trips are also possible, either by spotting a car or by arranging for a shuttle from the Dana Place—a courtesy extended to guests and sometimes to the public. Better yet, you can turn it into an all-day trip by picnicking at the Dollof farm or lunching at the Dana Place (meal service on weekends and holidays; snacks and fondue at other times). Finally, you can plan the tour as the Europeans do, tucking your worldly possessions into a pack and spending the night at this hostelry which

The Ellis River runs bright and free from Pinkham Notch to Jackson. ▶

9   Ellis River Trail

has been serving the wayfarer for more than a century. It's not exactly wilderness camping, but it does have its compensations.

Information and reservations: Dana Place, Jackson NH 03846. Telephone 603/383-6822.

10 Lowe's Bald Spot

To "summit" and return: 4 miles (8 miles possible)

Difficulty: moderate

Map: AMC Mt. Washington

Here's a taste of ski-mountaineering for anyone with a sturdy snowplow and a willingness to scramble about on snow. The view is fabulous, and somehow it's enhanced by the fact that you're standing inside a genuine wilderness reserve. Lowe's Bald Spot is a semi-alpine summit, so be prepared for bitter weather. (Charles Lowe was a mountain guide who cut several trails in the Northern Presidentials. History does not record whether or not he was bald.) Because it's located just inside the Great Gulf Wilderness, you must obtain a permit before you set out. Begin your trek at Pinkham Notch Camp, operated within the National Forest by the Appalachian Mountain Club; here you can obtain food, lodging, trail information, some supplies, and the necessary wilderness permit. The AMC complex is on the left as you drive north through Pinkham Notch on NH 16. There is ample parking for transients.

Directly behind the main building, Tuckerman Ravine Trail heads northwest beneath a sign warning hikers not to expect shelter on the summit of Mount Washington. Follow this trail for 100 yards, then ski to the right on the

Overleaf: Mount Adams as seen from the wind-scoured summit of Lowe's Bald Spot.

10   Lowe's Bald Spot

Old Jackson Road—a link in the famous Appalachian Trail from Georgia to Maine. It's a narrow path, marked by white blazes and discs at frequent intervals. After crossing the Blanchard Loop twice, it swings to the left and climbs rather steeply for about ⅓ mile. Then it levels off and even loses some altitude before climbing sharply again to join the Mount Washington Auto Road, 1⅔ miles from Pinkham Notch Camp. The road makes a sharp turn here, so you actually continue skiing in the same straight line.

In 100 yards, the road makes another sharp turn. Watch for white blazes on the trees to your right marking the

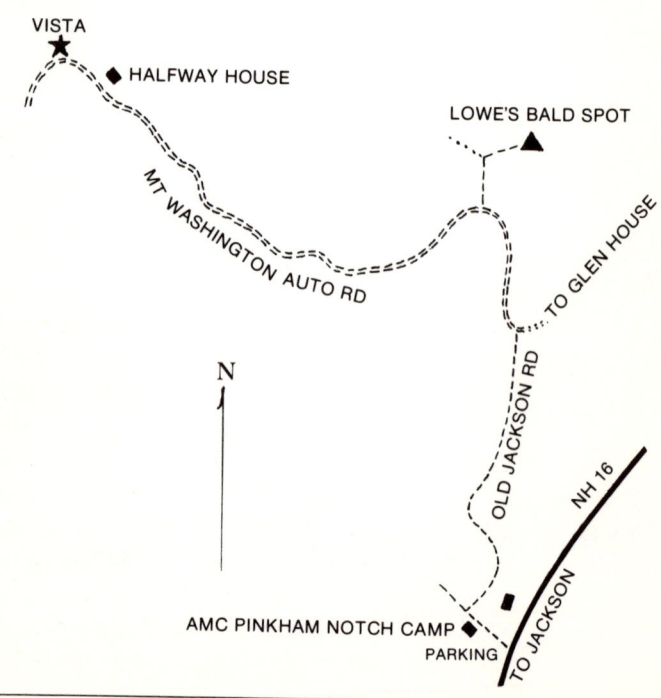

Lowe's Bald Spot

start of Madison Gulf Trail. Enter the woods here. You'll soon see the actual trail sign (people steal them if they're posted at roadside) and one of those Forest Service signs warning you of rigors ahead. The trail is not blazed but is hard to lose. It climbs steeply to a little pass; just after it levels off, watch for an AMC sign indicating that Madison Gulf Trail goes to the left and that Lowe's Bald Spot is uphill on the right. Take off your skis for the short scramble to the top, but carry them with you for added mobility and safety when you're on top.

You're virtually at tree-line, though the altitude is less than 3,000 feet. The big mountain is hidden by its own eastern flank, but there's an unequaled view of the Northern Presidentials—pyramid-shaped Mount Adams and ponderous Mount Madison. The Great Gulf separates you from them. Southwest is Boott Spur, a gorgeous jumble of rock and snow. Across the highway to the east is the Carter-Moriah Range and the Wildcat mountains (the one scarred by ski trails is Wildcat "D").

Return to the road as you came. If snow and weather conditions are favorable, you'll probably want to ski up the road for a mile or two. It's never too steep for properly-waxed skis, but the climb (and the descent!) is much more pleasurable after a recent snowfall. Otherwise the surface is likely to be rutted by the vehicles which carry men and supplies to the summit buildings. Skiing is often possible to Halfway House and usually impossible beyond, for this building is located at treeline; above it, the wind scours the road until nothing is left but ice and bare pavement. If you walk up another 100 yards or so, you'll be at the 4-mile marker, where there are views to rival those at Lowe's Bald Spot. The elevation here is about 4,000 feet—the same as that of Wildcat ski area across the way.

10 Lowe's Bald Spot

Skiing down the auto road—given a few inches of soft snow—is an experience to savor. Watch for the Old Jackson Road on your right, after a sharp turn to the right. This leg of the journey is somewhat less glorious. You must hold a snowplow for an interminable distance or else take your chances among the trees to one side or the other. Don't lose heart. Hot coffee awaits you at Pinkham Notch Camp.

11 Wildcat Valley Run

Summit to highway:
8½ miles

Difficulty: considerable

Map: Jackson Ski Touring

With good reason, the Wildcat Valley Trail has in a very few years become one of the most famous ski runs in the Northeast. As originally cut, it ran nearly 10 miles from the gondola station on Wildcat Mountain, clinging to the east side of the ridge for almost half its distance before dropping down into the valley and following Carter Notch Road to Jackson village. Most people now combine the upper half of this run with the Dana Place Trail. The variant is a bit shorter and saves many miles of over-the-highway travel, and it keeps you in the backcountry all the way.

The trail drops 2,950 vertical feet—more than you will encounter at any "downhill" ski resort in New Hampshire. Nevertheless, it was designed with cross-country skiers in mind, and it can be negotiated by anyone with a nimble step-turn and a snowplow that refuses to quit. There's an element of danger, to be sure, but it comes not from the skiing but from the fact that you're starting at the far end, so to speak. Once you've committed yourself to the trail, it's just not feasible to turn back. You would be well advised, therefore, to have at least three skiers in your party, and to carry a sleeping bag in case one of you is hurt and must wait several hours for help to arrive.

Hall's Ledge—the ultimate picnic spot, with Mount Washington beyond and the sun calling for a softer wax.

11 Wildcat Valley Run

You'll also need an extra automobile. Leave it at the Dana Place inn on NH 16, where there is a special parking lot for skiers; then drive 7 miles north to the Wildcat ski area. (Arrive early on weekends and holidays, or you will find the parking lot full and the lift-line stretching for a hundred yards.) Follow the downhill skiers to the ticket window and ask for a single-ride ticket on the gondola, costing $3 at this writing. You can expect some curious stares when you line up for one of the egg-shaped gondola cars, and again at the summit station when you head off for the "wrong" side of the mountain.

The trail begins directly behind the summit building, on a downslope rather tricky for cross-country skis. You'll see a sign down there and another where the trail shoots into the woods at your right. You're standing almost at treeline, and both the evergreens and the hardwoods are stunted by the harsh climate of this 4,000-foot ridge.

After entering the woods, the trail immediately switches back to the left, and it makes another zigzag soon after. Then it straightens out for a challenging but pleasant run, nearly 1½ miles to a first-aid cache on the right. More switchbacks follow, but they aren't as serious as those at the top. The trail then drops steeply through a hardwood grove (watch for the yellow diamonds marking the route) before leveling out and even climbing for a time. It then joins the logging-road network that it will follow for most of the remaining distance. Don't relax yet, however, for there's a sustained downhill run that will test your snowplow technique to the utmost. Take a break at Hall's Ledge, about 3 miles from the start and reached by a side-trail (#23) less than ¼ mile in length. It offers a stupendous view of Mount Washington, a sunny spot for a picnic, and a place to rest before resuming that interminable snowplow run.

11 Wildcat Valley Run

About 4 miles from the start, you'll leave the Wildcat Valley Trail (#46 in the Jackson system) for the Dana Place Trail (#9). This is beautiful touring country, rolling out to the west on what is almost a plateau. The miles pass swiftly here, but stay alert for the yellow markers: there are several junctions with logging roads other than the one that is your route, and some of these may have been skied. Finally you enter a region of mature spruce and hardwoods, where the trail veers northward. The Rocky Branch Ridge is visible through the trees to the west. Toward the end, the Dana Place Trail plunges downhill in fine style, as steep as anything you've encountered thus far. But the woods are open, so you'll know what lies

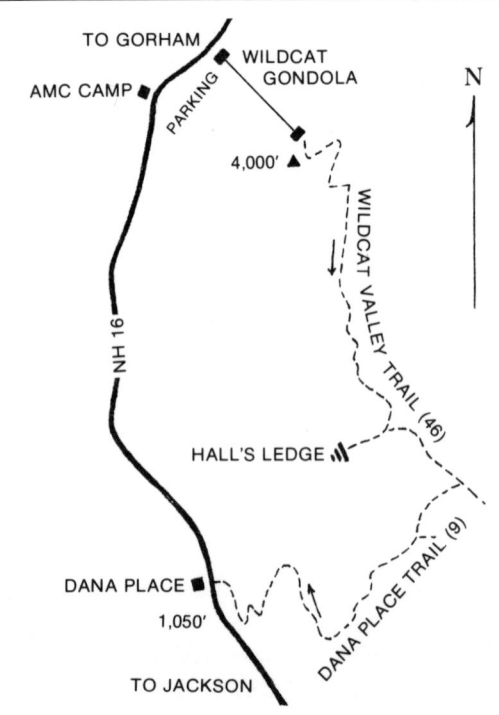

11 Wildcat Valley Run

ahead, and it's even possible to ski off the trail if you don't like the look of it.

After one final switchback, the trail slabs the mountainside within sound and sometimes sight of NH 16. It ends at the highway directly across from the Dana Place, where you can celebrate the end of one of the prettiest and most exciting ski runs you'll ever encounter.

Note: Early each March, skiers take part in a Wildcat Valley Run for the benefit of the N.H. Easter Seal Society. A guide and a naturalist accompany each group of about 10 skiers, so it's a very nice introduction to the route. Information from the Jackson Ski Touring Foundation, Box 90, Jackson NH 03846.

12 Mount Willard

To summit and return: 3 miles

Difficulty: considerable

MAP: AMC Mt. Washington

Like the people who compile dictionaries, those who edit the *AMC White Mountain Guide* rarely allow enthusiasm to run away with them. So it comes as something of a surprise to find a sentence like this: "From perhaps no other point in the mountains can so grand a view be obtained with so little effort." The point in question is the summit of Mount Willard, and the view is the deep gorge of Crawford Notch, walled on one side by the Webster Cliffs and on the other by Mount Willey of tragic fame. Neither words nor photographs can do it justice.

A word of caution: the AMC editors had the summer hiking trail in mind. For skiers, the view does not come so effortlessly. There's a stretch too steep to ski without climbing aids and too narrow for a sidestep or even a herringbone. The only answer is to take the old sealskins out of the attic, if you have them—or to resign yourself to walking part of the way.

The trailhead is located at the northern gate of Crawford Notch, near the point where US 302, the Maine Central Railroad, and Saco River compete for room between the perpendicular rocks. (As is usually the case when nature

Stormbound on the summit ledges of Mount Willard, high above Crawford Notch.

Mount Willard

stands in the way of progress, the Saco lost out. It's now buried in a culvert at the gate of the notch.) You'll see a highway marker, pointing somewhat inaccurately to Mount Willard; the trailhead sign is just behind it but may be obscured by the snowbanks. The easiest parking is to be found at the old Crawford railroad station, where you can cross the Maine Central tracks without climbing an embankment. Ski alongside the tracks for about 100 yards toward the notch, until you're abreast of the Mount Willard signs. Then turn at a right angle and ski straight across a meadow toward the most dramatic summit in view. This is Mount Tom, named for one of the eight sons of Abel Crawford, who settled this part of the country toward the end of the eighteenth century.

Tom Crawford kept the Notch House, located just across the highway from your departure point. In 1846 he cut a carriage road to the summit of Mount Willard for the entertainment of his guests, including Queen Victoria's maid of honor. "The ascent was really a tremendous one for any vehicle whatever," this lady reported; "and how we ever got safely up and down is a mystery to me." Anthony Trollope also passed this way, but he chose to walk.

As you enter the woods, a sign marks the junction of the Mount Willard Trail with one coming in from the right. Ski straight ahead, rather steeply uphill. In about 100 yards the summer hiking trail forks to the right and the carriage road to the left. The carriage road is the traditional route for winter climbers, because the grade is less severe. It has one badly washed-out portion which requires a light step to cross when the snow is soft, and which continues as a gully for 100 yards or more. After that, however, it improves considerably.

12 Mount Willard

Two turns later, the trail narrows and the trees become less stately, and you realize that the world is about to open before you. Use *extreme caution* when you go out on the summit ledges, which are narrow where the trail emerges and may be icy or windpacked. Keep close to the trees and move along to your right, where you'll find more room to maneuver. We arrived in a blizzard, with the Webster Cliffs and Mount Willey vanishing periodically into the storm. Still we could trace the highway and the railroad as they snaked down to the Willey Site, swept by a landslide in 1826. Green ice hung like a glacier over the Maine Central tracks. It was hard to imagine driving a train through Crawford Notch—let alone building the railroad in the first place.

The return trip proved easier than the ascent, for in the gully we could simply ski up the wall, sideslip to the bottom, and repeat. Lower down we skied a zigzag course through the trees. Any intermediate skier can handle the descent, and the view is reward enough for the troubles you encountered on the way up.

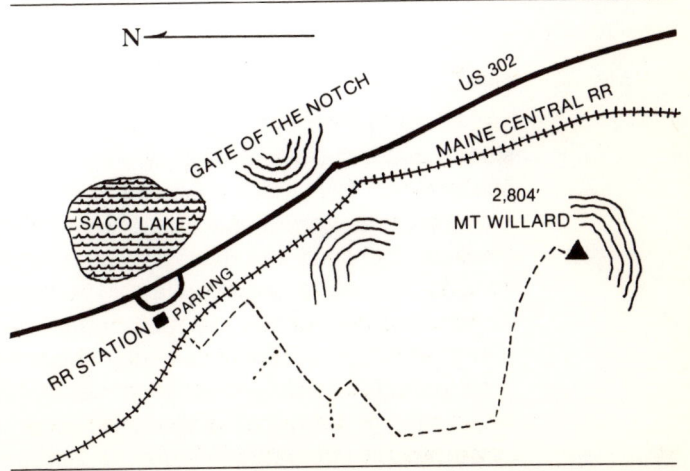

13 Ammonoosuc Loop

Around the loop: 4½ miles

Difficulty: slight

Map: AMC Mt. Washington

The Bretton Woods resort comes equipped with a grand hotel, an alpine ski area, 10,000 acres of land, a glorious view, and a highly uncertain future. Because of that last feature, we almost omitted it from these "25 Tours." But the view prevailed—that and the table-flat intervale behind the Mount Washington Hotel, where you can exhibit your best kick-and-glide beneath the mighty ramparts of the Presidential Range. There are few skiing experiences to equal it, so we'll hope that the "Sports Village at Bretton Woods"—once intended to be a second-home city of 20,000 inhabitants—will not change drastically in the next few years.

There's no mistaking the Mount Washington Hotel. It's just about the last of the grand old hostelries, white stucco and red tile and long verandas, located on US 302 between Twin Mountain and Crawford Notch. In fact, it's debatable which has caused more hearts to quicken—the snow-covered summits beyond or the hotel that was named for the mightiest of them. Impossible to winterize its ballroom-sized lobby and its endless corridors, so the hotel shuts down after Labor Day. The entry road is plowed, however. Drive along its stately length, where six-horse coaches once rolled with their cargo of Edwardian ladies and gentlemen.

13 Ammonoosuc Loop

The entry road forks before reaching the hotel; bear right for the touring center. The fee at this writing was $2 per person, including a sketch map of the trail system behind the hotel, another up on the slope of Little Mount Deception, and a third across the highway on the Rosebrook Mountains—82 kilometers altogether. (At Bretton Woods, all distances are metric. Thus the Ammonoosuc Loop is reckoned locally at 7.2 km.) There's a warming hut with an ornate parlor stove and a retail-rental shop. As elsewhere on the trail, the toilet consists of one of those green cubicles seen at urban construction sites.

For the Ammonoosuc Loop, ski straight ahead on the road you have followed thus far; unplowed now, it takes you

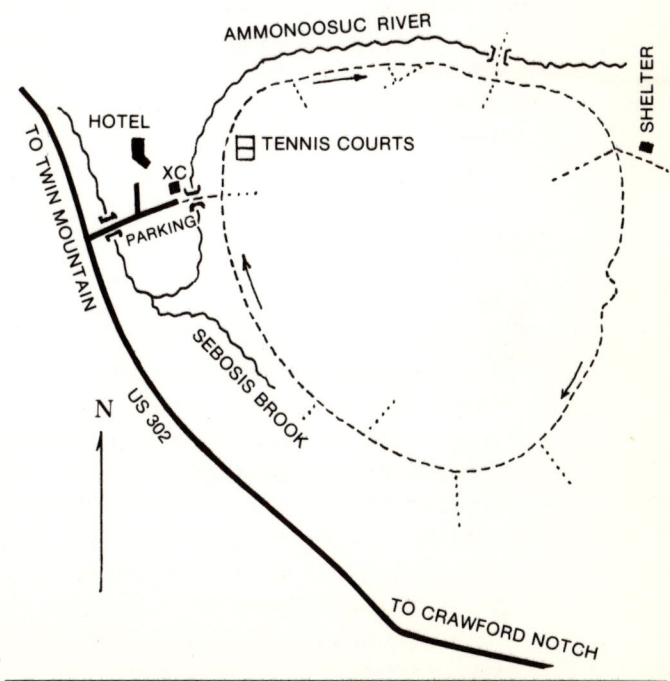

13 Ammonoosuc Loop

across a bridge and into an open field. After absorbing the view, turn left and ski along the Ammonoosuc River, which will be your companion for the next 2 miles. (The river rises at the Lakes of the Clouds, on the south side of Mount Washington.) The first leg takes you between the hotel and the tennis courts; then you swing to the right and in short order enter the woods on a bridle path. There are a few brisk climbs and an occasional dip in the trail but nothing to trouble the heart of a sturdy novice.

Bear left at each intersection until you pass a mini-gorge where the Ammonoosuc has carved the rocks into fantastic shapes, 1¼ miles from the start. Just beyond, there's an intersection whose left branch provides access to the Cog Railway road and Little Mount Deception. Ski straight ahead at this junction and do the same at the next one, and you will shortly reach the side-trail to Ammonoosuc Shelter. This is a rustic lean-to, open to the east, and therefore with an unusual view of the Southern Presidentials, ridge upon ridge unfolding to the north. The shelter was well-supplied with firewood when we passed through. There was a plentiful supply of animal tracks as well, where the woods creatures had come to dine on picnic leftovers.

The trail beyond the shelter is rough and leads only to the heavily-snowmobiled Mount Clinton Road. Return instead to the main trail and bear left. You'll discover that you've been gaining altitude all this while: there are some lovely downhill stretches, with an occasional turn to make them even more interesting. The trail then levels out and takes you through a cut-over area with a view of the Rosebrook Mountains to the southwest. Bear gradually to the right along the route of Sebosis Brook; soon you'll emerge from the woods with the Mount Washington

13   Ammonoosuc Loop

Hotel and Little Mount Deception straight ahead. Ski toward the hotel until you rejoin your outbound trail at the bridge over the Ammonoosuc, where the parking lot and touring center will be in sight.

Heaped with snow, Ammonoosuc Shelter provides a snug refuge and a splendid view.

14 Zealand Falls Hut

To hut and return:
13½ miles

Difficulty: moderate

Map: AMC Franconia

This is an overnight trip, courtesy of the Appalachian Mountain Club, which operates a number of "huts" or hostels in the White Mountains. The hut at Zealand Falls was the first to be adapted for winter use, opening a whole new world for the skier who wants to spend more than one day in the backcountry but isn't interested in the rigors of winter camping. Zealand Falls Hut is tucked on a hillside, overlooking a large pond which has the remarkable feature of feeding streams at both ends. The southeastern outlet flows down through Zealand Notch, a three-mile cut between cliffs scarred by avalanches and long-ago forest fires. It's a grand sight on a winter's morning.

The trail leaves from Zealand Campground 2½ miles east of Twin Mountain on US 302. The campground is not open during the winter, but the Forest Service keeps a parking area clear for wilderness travelers, on the other side of the highway and a couple hundred yards to the east. The first leg of the journey is due south on the Zealand Road—wide, evenly graded, and much traveled by snowmobiles. In a bit less than 4 miles, the road ends at Hoxie Brook. There is a sign here for Zealand Trail, which is closed to snowmobile traffic.

14   Zealand Falls Hut

Zealand Trail follows an old logging railroad for the most part, though second growth has narrowed it and there are no bridges over the streambeds. Nevertheless the grade is ideal for skiing. About 6 miles from the highway you will encounter a frozen marsh, where there may be beaver holes in the ice. (The summer trail swings around to the left, with Ethan Pond Trail coming in from the southeast just before reaching the hut. Winter traffic tends to cut across the marshy ground, avoiding the dog-leg and trail junction.) Soon after you leave the ice, Zealand Trail climbs steeply for 100 yards. If the snow is deep, you'll have to sidestep this section. Otherwise just

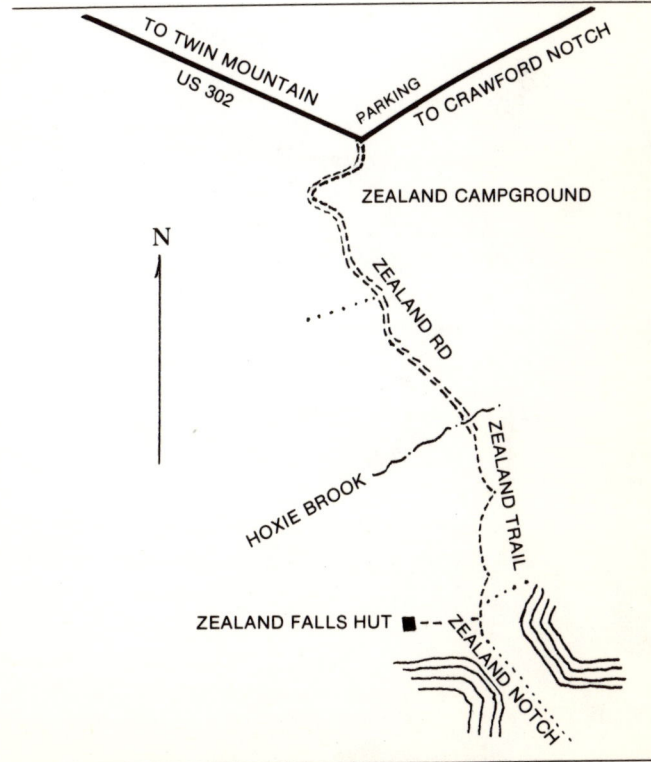

Zealand Falls Hut

take off your skis and carry them to Zealand Falls Hut. Highway to hostel, the distance is 6.3 miles; the average party should allow four hours for the climb, meaning that you should be on the trail before noon.

The hutmaster is in residence every night, although he or she may be absent when you arrive, skiing for pleasure

Zealand Falls Hut is nearly seven miles from the highway but offers most of the comforts of home.

Zealand Falls Hut

or for business. (One recent winter, the hutmaster chores were shared by a newlywed couple.) The winter huts do not provide food or blankets; fuel and water are rationed like the precious commodities they are. You cook on the hut's propane stove, and you are welcome to use the utensils and tableware also, if you wash them afterward. The bunkrooms have been known to reach sub-zero temperatures by morning, so a good sleeping bag is essential. The sanitary facilities consist of his-and-her outhouses.

Zealand Falls Hut is generally crowded on weekends and holidays, often to its capacity of 36. It is frequently empty during the week. The overnight fee reflects this pattern, being higher on the high-use days—but a bargain at any time. (We paid $3 each on a weekday; the rate for Fridays, Saturdays, and holiday weeks was $6 a night.) Reservations are required.

Next morning you can ski out the way you came—an almost perfect hour's run for an intermediate skier—or you can take day trips ranging from the mild to the hazardous. The easiest of these is a jaunt down through Zealand Notch to Thoreau Falls, 6 miles roundtrip. A strong intermediate party can ski out to US 302 via Ethan Pond Trail, covering the 8 miles in about four hours. And—for experts only—there is a trek south to the Kancamagus Highway, involving 14 miles and a full day's work. Seek the hutmaster's advice before you attempt any of these tours.

Information and reservations: AMC Pinkham Notch Camp, Gorham NH 03581. Telephone (603) 466-2727.

15 The Inns of Franconia

To inn and return: 7½ miles

Difficulty: moderate

Map: AMC Franconia

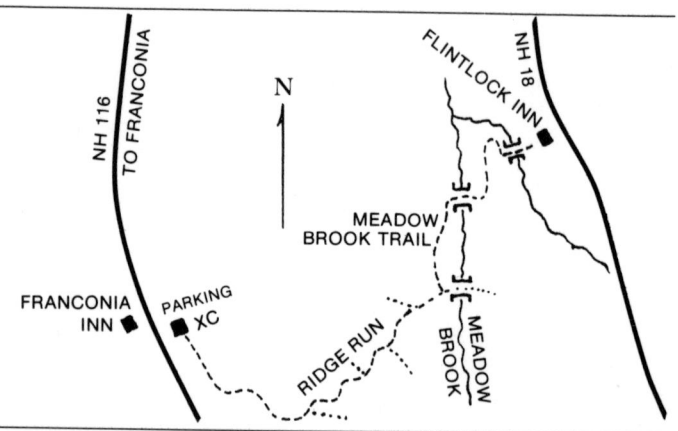

Here is a tour for a stormy day. It takes you through woodlands for all but the first hundred yards or so, and it breaks for lunch at a ski lodge with a roaring fire and a reasonable menu.

One of the oldest ski towns in New Hampshire, Franconia was slow to adapt to the touring revolution of the 1970s. When it caught up, however, it did so with a rush. Virtually all the scattered lodges of Franconia (and even Sugar Hill to the west) are now linked by cross-country trails, and you can even go a-touring to the downhill resorts of Mittersill and Cannon Mountain. The town is

15   The Inns of Franconia

reached via Exit 38 on Interstate 93. As you enter the village, however, continue straight ahead on Church Street (NH 116) instead of turning right for the shopping district. There is a large chamber-of-commerce directory at this intersection: follow the arrow to Easton, the Franconia Inn, and the airport.

In just over 2 miles you'll see the inn on your right and a tennis center on the left. Just beyond the tennis center is the ski-touring shop, which at this writing consisted of two office trailers joined at right angles. Rental equipment, lessons, and guided tours are available here. (The Franconia trails aren't shown on the AMC sheet. You might want to draw in the route from our sketch map, so you'll know where you stand with respect to the neighboring mountains.) The trail you want is Ridge Run. To find it, ski toward Cannon Mountain and its skein of downhill trails, then skirt the woods until you reach the second major trailhead. It's marked by a yellow sign bearing its name, plus a sign for the Flintlock Inn, which is your destination.

These are relatively new woods, so the trees are closely spaced. Ridge Run follows an extremely crooked path through the trees, mostly evergreen to begin with but giving way to hardwood as you climb to the top of the ridge. The change in altitude is little more than 300 feet, but the narrow trail and the frequent changes of direction require that both your mind and your feet be nimble. Each turn is signaled by a yellow arrow. About ½ mile from the start, Cliffhanger leaves on the right, and at about 1 mile Shortcut leaves on the left, both trails marked by red signs. Then Ridge Run heads steeply downhill to its second junction with Cliffhanger. The woods are mostly evergreen again. Middle Earth trail is on your left,

The Inns of Franconia

marked by a blue sign, and soon you pick up Meadow Brook on your right. From here the trail is virtually flat.

Ridge Run ends at a very narrow bridge over Meadow Brook, 2½ miles from the start, where a side-trail leads to Lovett's Inn and the Horse and Hound. Keep bearing to the left on Meadow Brook Trail, which leads you away from the stream and then back to it, crossing to the east bank on a more substantial bridge. The trail now passes through what looks like marshy ground—indeed, it follows a stream bed for a distance—until you spot houses through the trees on your right. Abruptly, you come out on the bank of Lafayette Brook, rushing down toward its rendezvous with the Gale River, the Ammonoosuc, and eventually the Connecticut, which will empty the melting snows of Franconia into Long Island Sound.

The Flintlock Inn is just across the river and is reached by a footbridge erected for this purpose. Like most of the lodges in Franconia, the Flintlock has seen better days, but the fare is substantial, reasonably priced, and pleasantly served.

On the return trip, oddly enough, the trail is harder to follow. Once over the ridge we kept bearing off on side-trails to the right which weren't visible when we were outward bound. However, they all led to the same place in the end, and we left the woods as we had entered them, but with the stormclouds blowing away to give us a stupendous view of Cannon Mountain, the lesser summits known as the Cannon Balls, and mighty Kinsman to the south.

◀ Bridges are put up each winter to link the inns of Franconia, including the Flintlock across Lafayette Brook.

16 The Old Man

To tramway and return: 4½ miles

Difficulty: moderate

MAP: AMC Franconia

The Old Man of the Mountains is probably the most famous rock formation in the world. Nathaniel Hawthorne wrote him into American literature, Daniel Webster praised him in words enshrined in *Bartlett's Familiar Quotations,* and the New Hampshire liquor commission adapted him for a souvenir whiskey bottle. Here is your chance to become acquainted with the Profile. Skiing through Franconia Notch, you will see the ledges of Cannon Mountain first as a jumble of rock, then as a vague human likeness, and finally as the perfect and forbidding features of a stern old man.

The tour begins at Lafayette Campground, 2¾ miles from the state park entrance as you drive north on US 3. The campground sign is removed in the winter months, but the signpost is still there and the road is plowed wide to accomodate climbers on the Old Bridle Path (on the right). The campground entrance road (on the left) is also plowed with ample parking space. To reach the trailhead, ski toward the park headquarters building. Immediately after crossing the bridge, turn right for the Profile Lake Trail. It is marked by a sign and closely follows the infant Pemigewasset River.

Soon after leaving the campground, you'll cross to the

Young skier surveys the Old Man of the Mountains, perched 1,200 feet above Profile Lake. ▶

right bank on a footbridge; the path then climbs to higher ground. The topographical maps and trail descriptions suggest that this route is almost flat, but in truth it climbs and dips in quite a busy fashion as it tries to find a foothold between the highway and the river. A summer hiker would take little notice of these changes in elevation, but for a skier on a narrow trail they pose more of a challenge.

As you ski along, the Cannon Cliffs take definite shape on your left, and Eagle Cliff appears almost straight ahead. Watch for a patch of brown ledge at the northern end of Cannon Cliffs: this will eventually be transformed into the Old Man of the Mountains. About 1 mile from the start, you'll recross the Pemigewasset on another footbridge, at a point where rock-climbers come in from the highway for their assaults on the Cannon Cliffs. A sign-out box has been provided for them at the bridge. For you, the trail continues on the left bank all the way to Profile Lake, at the outlet of which you should cross back

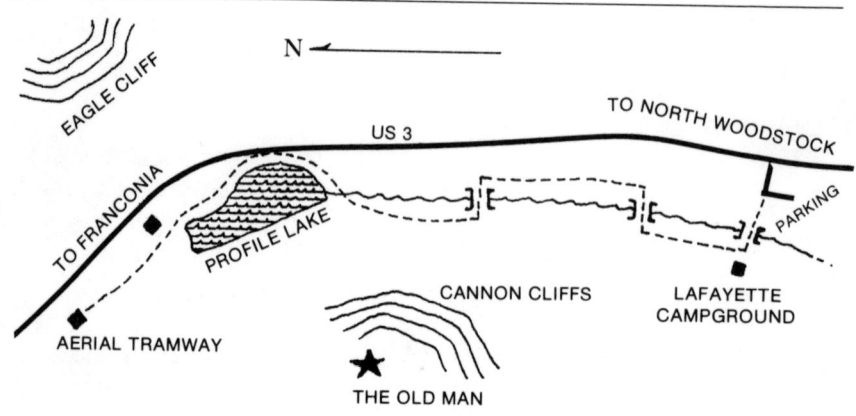

The Old Man

to the other shore. This crossing was marked by bamboo wands when we passed through.

There are two reasons for skiing up the east bank of Profile Lake: to take advantage of level terrain and to get the best perspective on the Old Man. The path enters a scrubby woods, close by the lake, where considerable snow is necessary to cover the rocks and roots. Ice permitting, you can also ski along the lake, close to the shore.

The profile first appears, in the words of a nineteenth-century writer, as "a toothless old woman in a mob cap." But in the space of 100 yards his jaw firms up, his brow begins to beetle, and he becomes the Old Man of picture-postcard fame. Three ledges combine to form this optical illusion. The profile is 40 feet tall, and might have fallen long since if it hadn't been repaired by steel rods and epoxy cement. The man who alerted New Hampshire to the fact that its symbol was endangered was the Rev. Guy Roberts. Major repairs were made in the 1920s and again in the 1950s. There is a plaque in Roberts' honor at the point where the profile appears to best advantage.

To reach the tramway station, ski behind a summer gift shop and across the unplowed Profile Lake parking lot. A sign for the Aerial Tramway will then be visible beside the highway. The state-operated building provides cafeteria service and a warm place to rest.

Skiing back the way you came, take note of the eastern wall of Franconia Notch, scarred by the landslides which have closed the highway for days and even weeks at a time. The largest came down in 1948, and its track was widened by another slide in 1959.

17 Flume Gorge

To gorge and return:
1½ miles

Difficulty: slight

Map: AMC Franconia

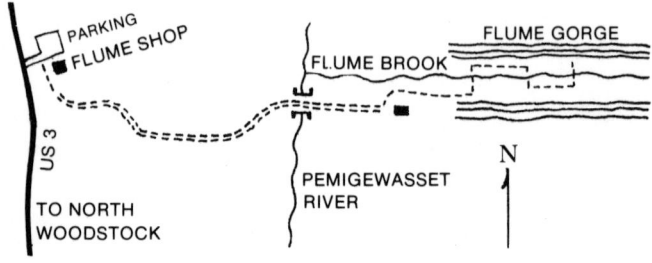

Franconia Notch was whittled to its present remarkable shape by a mile-high sheet of ice, which scoured the walls as it advanced and retreated. The job was finished some 10,000 years ago, but escaped public notice until well into the nineteenth century. It wasn't until 1813 that the state built a road through the notch, and it wasn't until 1826 that a newspaper saw fit to mention this beautiful cleft in the mountains. Shortly thereafter, the first tourists appeared in Franconia Notch—a trickle that became a flood. The burden is now so great (up to 16,000 cars per day) as to threaten changes more drastic than any since the Ice Age came and went.

Among the great attractions in Franconia Notch is the Flume, a gorge discovered by an elderly fisherwoman, Jessie Guernsey, circa 1808. During the summer and fall, the New Hampshire Division of Parks does a brisk

17 Flume Gorge

business selling admission tickets and bus rides to the tourists. In the winter, however, the turnstiles fall silent. And that's ironical, because it's in the winter that the gorge takes on its most spectacular covering. The granite walls are cased with ice—blue, green, gray, and brown—the largest icicles you may ever be privileged to see. Don't miss this tour, whether you be novice or ski-mountaineer.

Driving north on US 3, you will see the green Flume Shop on the right, ¾ mile after you enter the state park. The entryway is plowed. This trek is very popular with snowshoers, however, and there may be some competition for the dozen spaces that are available in the winter parking lot. Ski directly in front of the Flume Shop and through the turnstile gate, beneath a sign reading "The Flume and Pool." This manuever will take you onto the graded road which carries tourist busses during the summer—for skiers, a route much more desirable than the hiking path. The road goes straight ahead for a short distance, paralleling the highway, then turns eastward toward the Franconia mountains. The view of these summits—Liberty, Flume, and Whaleback—gets progressively more dramatic as you ski along. The route is mostly downhill, with two fairly steep pitches, both of them with ample runout.

At the bottom of the second incline is the Pemigewasset River and one of the prettiest covered bridges in New Hampshire. The bridge was built about 1820. A relatively short span, it uses the simplest of all truss designs, a "multiple kingpost" in which the downward forces are transmitted from one post to its neighbor by a slanting beam mortised into the top of it. (Covered bridges were covered in order to keep the trusswork from rotting.) As you pass through the bridge, you will find yourself skiing

17   Flume Gorge

17 Flume Gorge

on dry boards. In the old days, the town fathers arranged for snow to be shoveled into such bridges, so sleighs could pass through them without difficulty.

The road now climbs briefly and ends at another park building, ½ mile from the start. If the traffic has been at all heavy, you will probably find it much easier to leave your skis here and proceed on foot, taking your poles for balance. The path skirts the right bank of Flume Brook, occasionally visible through holes in the ice. At the first footbridge, stay on the right bank and continue straight ahead, entering the gorge. From here on the route follows the summer boardwalk, crossing and recrossing the stream on bridges. It's usually possible to go upstream as far as the third bridge, after which the boardwalk has been taken up to save it from washing out in the spring. *Caution:* do not venture onto the ice. You can already see the best part of the gorge, with its sheer walls of Conway granite, 70 feet tall and 10 to 20 feet apart.

The Flume resulted from what geologists call a "dike"—a seam of lava left here in the Age of Fire that preceded the Age of Ice. The granite was split open by the molten rock; the crack was filled by the softer stone; and this "dike" was gradually worn away by the gurgling waters of the stream we now call Flume Brook.

◄ Encrusted with ice, Flume Gorge is even more spectacular in winter than in the tourist season.

18 Wilderness Trail

To campsite and return: 5½ miles (11 miles possible)

Difficulty: slight

Map: AMC Franconia

Despite its name—indeed, largely because of its name—the Wilderness Trail is one of the most civilized backcountry tours imaginable. So many people follow this route that the Forest Service has seen fit to divide the trail, giving the right lane to snowshoers and pedestrians, the left lane to skiers. (The snowmobiles, meanwhile, have their own parallel trail on the other side of the river.) This divided-highway approach is possible because the Wilderness Trail follows the bed of the old East Branch & Lincoln Railroad, which once carried three trains a day to the pulp mill downriver, each laden with 7,000 board feet of virgin spruce.

To reach the trailhead, leave Interstate 93 at Exit 32 and drive 5 miles east on NH 112—the Kancamagus Highway. The road passes first through Lincoln, where the old pulp mill still leads an off-again, on-again existence. Next there's the Loon Mountain ski area, which keeps one of the original EB&LRR locomotives on display. Just before the road crosses the East Branch on a concrete bridge, you'll see the trailhead parking lot on your left. There's no mistaking it, for even on weekdays several cars are likely to be parked here.

18 Wilderness Trail

The ski route heads north along the East Branch of the Pemigewasset and very often within view of it. The East Branch drains a vast tract of country known to history as the Pemigewasset Wilderness and to the Forest Service as the Pemigewasset Unit. Whatever the name, this land is a tribute to the recuperative powers of nature. When men discovered how to make paper out of wood pulp instead of expensive cotton, 35,000 acres were cut clean in half a generation, 1893 to 1907. Then the whole thing burned. The remnants of the Pemigewasset Wilderness were still being picked over in the 1940s—but already the forest is coming back. The only enduring monuments to the loggers are the clearings where they once lived, and the straight and level roadbed of the EB&LRR. Oc-

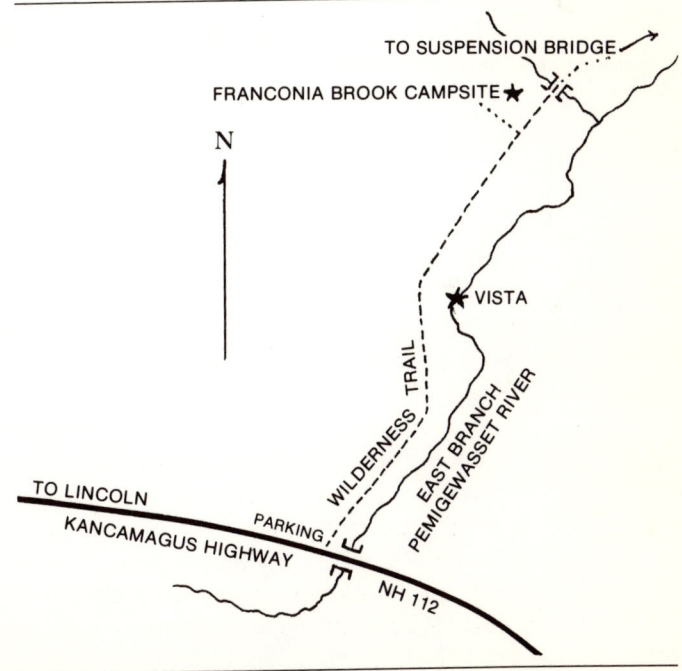

18 Wilderness Trail

Franconia Brook Shelter often serves as a base for winter tours of the Pemigewasset Wilderness.

casionally, too, you will see a telegraph pole along the railroad right-of-way.

About 1½ miles from the road, the trail passes so close to the East Branch that you can easily ski onto the river. Take the opportunity, for the view north to Bondcliff and West Bond will give you an idea of the scope and wildness of this country. The mountains to the east are the Hancocks. All of them were timbered off, except a few spots that were absolutely inaccessible or which fell under disputed ownership.

There's a signpost on the left side of the trail, 2½ miles from the road, where a side-trail leaves northwest to Black Pond. It's obscure in the winter, but worth following for 100 feet or so, after which you'll find yourself in a

Wilderness Trail

clearing with a view of the lower Franconia Ridge, with snow-capped Mount Liberty just visible on the right. Returning to the Wilderness Trail, you'll reach Franconia Brook campsite in about ¼ mile. There's a lovely shelter here, low-roofed and open to the east, and therefore empty of snow in most winters. If you have a yearning to try winter camping, this is a good place to begin—preferably not on a weekend, however. We met five campers on a Monday morning, one party from the shelter and another from a more distant campsite.

The Wilderness Trail crosses Franconia Brook on a narrow foot-bridge which utilizes the supports of the old railroad trestle. The trail continues on its level path for many miles beyond. If you want a farther destination, aim for the 180-foot suspension bridge where the Wilderness Trail crosses to the south bank of the river. This span is exciting enough in the summer; in the winter it can be terrifying. The distance from Franconia Brook campsite to the suspension bridge is 2¾ miles, for a total round-trip journey of 11 miles. We suggest you go no farther unless you are prepared to spend the night.

19 Peeling

To townsite and return: 2 miles (4–8 miles possible)

Difficulty: moderate

Map: AMC Franconia

How is it possible that a town could vanish from the face of the earth? Yet it happened to more than one mountain village in the second half of the nineteenth century—their young men killed in the Civil War or lured to the West, their pattern of life disrupted by such innovations as the stove, the sewing machine, and the railroad. Among these vanished towns was Peeling. Its boundaries still remain, enclosing the township we now call Woodstock, but of the original settlement nothing survives except cellar holes and stone walls. They can be found, even in winter, on the level heights of Mount Cilley, some two miles to the west of the highway that now runs through the settled portions of Woodstock.

The Mount Cilley Trail can be skied in either direction, but the climb is less arduous and the parking is easier if you take it from the west. From Interstate 93, take Exit 32 and make a right turn for North Woodstock and Lost River Road (NH 112). About 2½ miles beyond the traffic light, NH 118 leaves on the left. Follow this road for 1½ miles to the trail sign on your left; you'll have to park on the shoulder of the road, but there is usually plenty of room. Ski into the woods and downhill, watching the hardwood trunks for the scars that indicate a long-ago hatchet blaze: if there is no track, these will be your only guide

19 Peeling

for much of the way. The trail soon bears around to the right and crosses Jackman Brook at a point indicated by a sign, then follows the stream for a short distance before swinging off to the left and uphill. The going is steep for a time, then more gentle, with occasional orange diamonds to mark the route.

About ¾ mile from the start, you'll leave the hardwood forest and enter a region of tall spruce, as abruptly as if you were passing from one room to another. Shortly thereafter, the trail trends downhill for the first time to an intersection not shown on the AMC map. This is the old village square. The right fork is the original highway; given a snowmobile track to follow or a good eye for where the trail should go, you can ski it for about 1½ miles to Elbow Pond. There's at least one cellar hole, on the left, ⅓ mile from the village square.

Continuing straight ahead on the Mount Cilley Trail, you soon become conscious of skiing between stone walls, and in a few hundred feet a cellar hole is visible just off

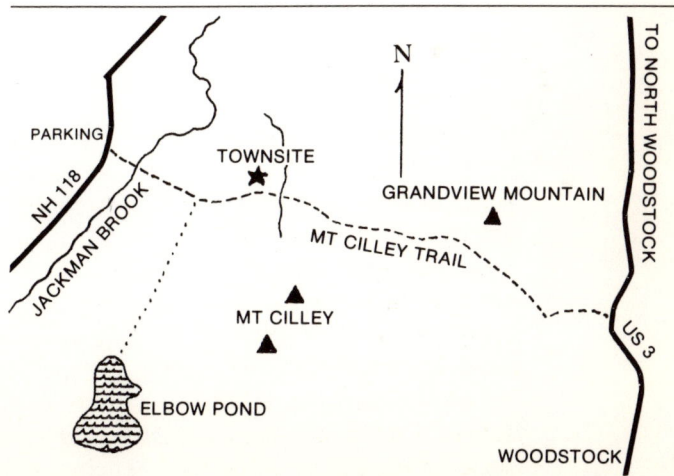

19 Peeling

19 Peeling

the trail on the left. This was the home of J. R. Smith during Peeling's short life as a community—first settled in 1773, abandoned soon after the Civil War. A short distance beyond, and also on the left, is the site of the Peeling school. According to a hand-lettered sign we found there, "20–30 scholars during the winter shivered around the old stone fireplace." We found other such signs. Just beyond the school, for example, we crossed a stream identified as "School House Brook—also known as Shirt Brook—Pa Smith washed his shirt here." (In the 1892 atlas of New Hampshire, the village and the highway had already disappeared, but this tributary of Jackman Brook was still shown as Shirt Brook.)

The trail continues up and down, crosses a more substantial stream, then climbs easily to its height-of-land on Grandview Mountain. There is no view these days, except of spruce trees reaching for the sunlight. You are now about halfway to US 3, and the trail henceforth is downhill almost all the way. If the snow conditions are favorable and your party is large enough, you might want to toss a coin to see who will go back to the car and who'll ski straight through. (The pick-up point is 3 miles from the traffic light in North Woodstock, just beyond a sign for Irma's Restaurant.) Consider that the track is not very wide, that it is occasionally steep, and that a compacted snowmobile trail can be both fast and difficult to ski on. Downhill, the trail is easy to follow until near the end, where it swings to the left and passes through the front yard of an A-frame cottage. *Slow down now,* or you'll find yourself shooting out onto the pavement of US 3.

◄ A cellar hole is all that remains of Pa Smith's house, in the heart of abandoned Peeling.

20 Tunnel Brook

To upper pond
and return:
11 miles

Difficulty:
moderate

Map: AMC
Franconia

The White Mountain landscape was shaped by violent forces, fire and ice being among the favored mechanisms. But gentler forces are also at work. Among them is the industrious beaver, creating meadows where once there was only a quiet brook among the rocks. One of the most extensive beaver-works we've ever seen is located at the head of Tunnel Brook, in the col between Mount Moosilauke and Mount Clough. It's a far distance on skis, but the traveling has been made easy by a Forest Service access road which now covers more than half the distance. (Naturally the road is popular with snowmobilers, too, so this tour is most pleasant on a weekday after new snow has fallen.)

Drive through Kinsman Notch on NH 112 (see previous tour). Nearly 9 miles from the traffic light in North Woodstock, and just as a red house comes into view ahead, make a left turn onto a plowed road. This is the Noxon Road, paved and plowed for about ½ mile. There is ample room to park at the end of the maintained section. Ski southward on the road for about 1 mile—gently uphill for the most part—until it crosses Tunnel Brook on a bridge. Here the Noxon Road doubles back to the north, while the Forest Service access road continues

20 Tunnel Brook

southward on the right bank of the stream. A sign identifies the route as Tunnel Brook Trail, although the old footpath has mostly vanished beneath the gravel and the guardrails. (At this writing, the AMC sheet did not show the access road, but the Tunnel Brook Trail was a sufficiently accurate representation of its route.) At first it follows close to the stream, but then it swings off to the right and begins to climb a shoulder of land, with the great hulk of Moosilauke ridge visible to the southeast. When you reach the high ground on this detour, you'll just be able to make out the col between Moosilauke and Clough where you are heading.

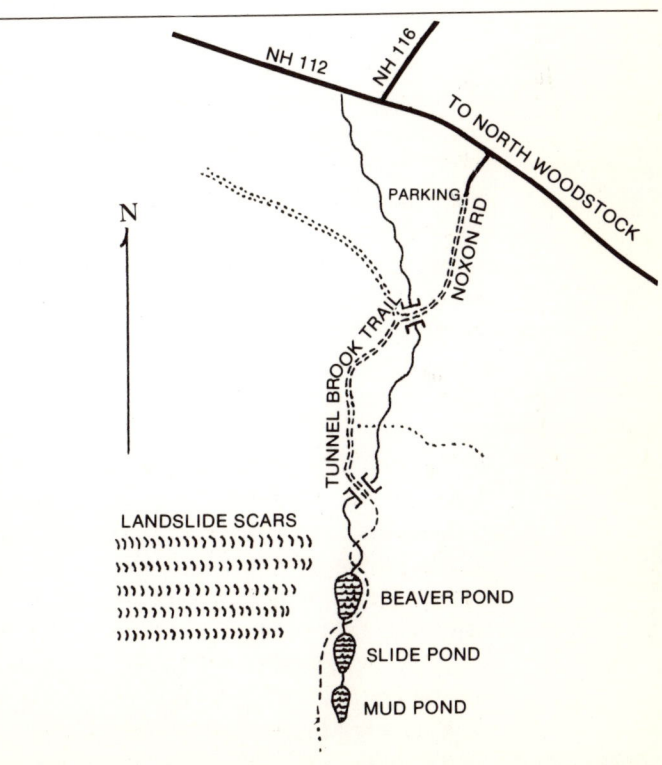

20 Tunnel Brook

The road returns to Tunnel Brook about 2¾ miles from the start, whereupon the Benton Trail leaves on the left. The road continues nearly ¾ mile more, crossing to the left bank on a bridge and ending at a parking lot for summer hikers. The footpath continues straight ahead through scrubby hardwoods, crossing several tributary streams and at one point making a sudden jog to the left. All the crossings are bridged, if only by a log or two. Eventually the trail returns to Tunnel Brook and follows it closely through young hemlock and fir; the scars of landslides are visible on Mount Clough ahead. Shortly thereafter you must cross to the right bank, follow a rough stretch near the slides, and cross back to the left bank again.

Abruptly, you emerge upon the beaver meadow and its succession of dams—an engineering marvel that covers 20 acres at this point, creating a shallow pond which apparently has no name. Where it narrows at the upper end, Tunnel Brook Trail crosses to the right bank on yet another dam, though a very short one. When we crossed over, we could see the engineers' muddy footprints on the snow and some tentative gnawing upon nearby saplings, as if the beaver were readying themselves for the spring breakup.

On the right bank now, Tunnel Brook Trail can be hard to follow at times. It passes Slide Pond, where avalanche scars are visible on Moosilauke as well as on Mount Clough; then it passes Mud Pond, where the stream rises. Both ponds have been dammed, apparently to control the amount of water flowing into the meadow to the north. Altogether, the beaver-works extend for ½ mile from the first dam to the final structure on Mud Pond, which is about 5½ miles from where you left your car.

Tunnel Brook Trail continues downhill from this point, joining the North-South Road near the town of Glencliff. The distance is just over 2 miles. Since the North-South Road is largely unplowed, a strong party could use it as the return leg to the Noxon Road, a triangular tour of approximately 17 miles. See the AMC Franconia sheet for details.

Row upon row of beaver dams have flooded the high ground between Moosilauke and Mount Clough.

21 Russell Pond

To pond and return: 8 miles

Difficulty: slight

Map: AMC Franconia

The Tripoli Road got its name from the diatomaceous earth—also called "tripoli"—that was mined near Thornton Gap just before World War I. Later, the abandoned access road was extended through the gap into Waterville Valley, creating a lovely route for motorists in the summer and snowmobilers in the winter. For skiers, the Tripoli Road serves as the introduction to a long but gentle tour to Russell Pond, where the Forest Service maintains a campground and recreation area. The trip is best scheduled after a snowfall has covered the ruts left by the tracked vehicles—and even by the jeeps that sometimes venture this way.

From Interstate 93, take Exit 31 and follow the sign that points to Russell Pond Campground. In a very short distance, the plowed road ends; park your car so that it does not block the right-of-way for other winter travelers. Skiing eastward on Tripoli Road, you soon enter the National Forest amid a welter of signs. (The oddest of these, when we passed through, declared that "National Forests Mean Winter Fun"—complete with a silhouette of an alpine skier powering through a turn.) The road continues its steady, gentle ascent until you reach the Russell Pond turnoff, 1¾ miles from the start.

21 Russell Pond

Russell Pond Road is on your left, boasts another of those massive Forest Service signs, and may be barred to traffic. The gate discourages some snowmobilers but by no means all of them. Scramble over or under it and begin the climb to Russell Pond—a steeper grade than you have been following, but with occasional switchbacks to keep matters from getting out of hand. At the first switchback, there is a fine view eastward toward Thornton Gap and Mount Tecumseh, whose far slope contains the alpine ski trails that have made Waterville Valley famous as a winter resort.

Toward the end of the access road there is another switchback, this one so tight as to deserve the title of hairpin turn. Just beyond it you'll find a turn-out for automobiles—and a most remarkable view. The southern mountains are spread out before you, so grand that you're certain their names must be familiar, but you must struggle with a compass and map before locating such odd-sounding peaks as Wanosha Mountain. (A USGS

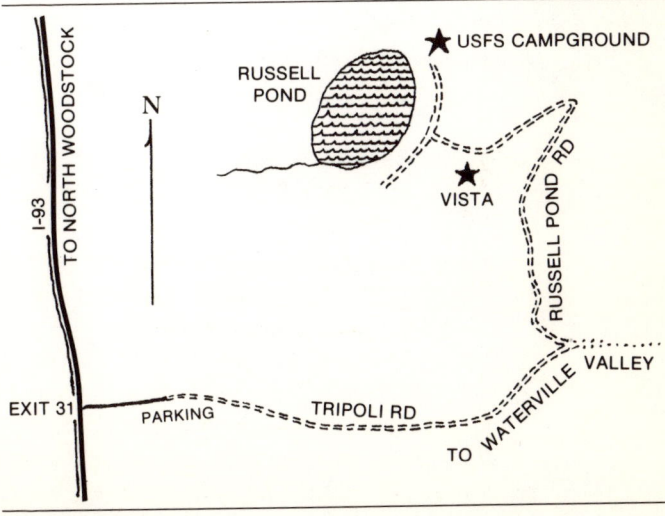

map or the AMC Waterville sheet is best for this purpose.) Eastward the task is easier. Thornton Gap is dramatically visible as the traditional U-shaped notch of the White Mountains, with Tecumseh to its south and Breadtray Ridge to the north.

Soon after the outlook—and 4 miles from where you left your car—Russell Pond Road tops out at an intersection. The left fork goes nowhere: it was intended to serve a picnic area on the west bank of Russell Pond, but this project was never finished. The right fork leads downhill to the Forest Service campground, now deserted for the winter. Its signs, buildings, and trash containers are rather unsightly after two hours in the snowy woods. However, ice permitting, you can leave them behind by skiing out to the pond itself. Use *extreme caution,* especially on the western shore where Russell Pond Brook flows out to its rendezvous with the Pemigewasset. We found open water here even after two sub-zero days. The best policy would be to let the snowmobilers show the way: if they don't break through the ice, you certainly won't.

For the most part, the woods around Russell Pond are too thick to explore on skis, so after circling the shoreline and eating lunch (at a picnic table if you're so inclined) there's nothing for it but to climb back to the height-of-land. Then it's downhill all the way, 2.2 miles to the Tripoli Road. For a memorable ride, put a coat of paraffin over your touring wax, crouch down, and enjoy the spectacle of yellow-and-black highway markers signaling you to turn left or right. There is one final sign reminding you to STOP. Heed it, for if the gate is closed you'll find it too high to jump and too low to ski beneath. Turn right on Tripoli Road, and you'll be back to your car in decidedly less time than you required for the upward journey.

◀ An unplowed road opens up the backcountry for touring that is fast and pleasant.

22 Peaked Hill Pond

To pond and return:
4½ miles

Difficulty: moderate

Map: AMC Chocorua-Waterville

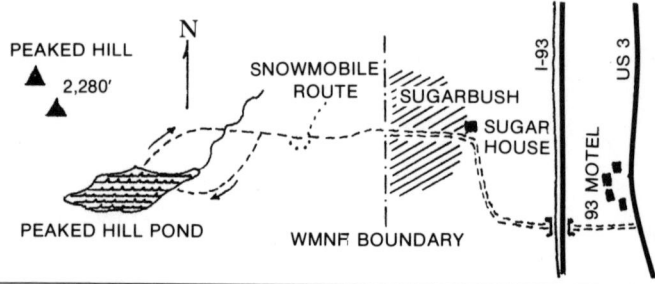

Unless you've always wanted to see a "sugarbush" at harvest time, you should plan this tour for the frigid months. When the maple sap begins to run—usually in March, but sometimes toward the end of February—the first mile will be plowed clean or churned up by the tracked vehicle used to tend the trees and to bring the sap down to the sugar house. It's quite a sight, but it does interfere with the skiing.

Peaked Hill (it's pronounced "peak-ed," by the way) is located in the town of Campton, which was split in half by the construction of Interstate 93. Driving north on the Interstate, take Exit 29 and make a left turn onto US 3. Follow the old highway north for just over 2 miles to the 93 Motel, a cluster of white buildings on the left. You'll see the trail sign at roadside just before the motel. Park in the motel lot—by permission—or along the shoulder of the road. Then ski uphill toward the Interstate, along a road constructed for the sole purpose of giving access to the sugarbush and through two tunnels which serve the same purpose. After passing under the southbound lanes, you'll swing to the right and parallel the Interstate for about ¼ mile. There is a directional sign here and another at the sugar house, ½ mile from the start.

The farm road through the sugarbush heads uphill to the left, following a compass course that is generally west-northwest. It's quite a substantial tract of maple, ending abruptly at the National Forest boundary, which is marked by the usual yellow sign, a stone wall, and (at least when we passed through) red streamers which presumably were meant to keep the snowmobilers out of the sugarbush. Soon after entering the National Forest, you'll find yourself skiing through a gorgeous stand of evergreens—pine, hemlock, spruce, and fir. We'd never before seen all four species growing so abundantly in the same stretch of woods.

This was farming country not too many years ago, and in a little more than 1 mile from the start you'll skirt the edge of an old pasture. You can obtain fair views by skiing through the pasture; the trail continues in the same westerly direction from its north side. Soon, however, the trail swings sharply to the left (an arrow marks the turning) and climbs steeply uphill to a junction with a snowmobile trail not shown on any map. Your route lies straight uphill, which is also where the snowmobilers are going. About 2 miles from the start you'll meet a pitiful spruce which has been spray-painted blue. Here the trail forks, with the snowmobile route going to the left and the summer footpath to the right. They both lead to the pond,

Peaked Hill keeps vigil over the lonely pond that was named for it.

22 Peaked Hill Pond

and you can use them to make a loop as shown on the sketch map. Going to the pond on the snowmobile track involves a level path for the most part, bearing around to the right and dropping down to a sort of picnic grove at the water's edge. This route is rather scrubby. The hiking path is much prettier, dropping down and then regaining the lost altitude as it swings around to the left.

Peaked Hill Pond is a small, sunny depression among the trees, well sheltered from any wind that may be blowing. There is beaver activity at the northern outlet where the trail crosses the ice. *Caution:* there may be holes where the beavers come up to forage and survey. A few dead trees indicate that these acquatic engineers have raised the water level in recent years, drowning part of the forest in the process. Due west is the hill from which the pond takes its name—peaked indeed! In fact, there seems to be a second peak behind the first, and from water level we couldn't judge which was the true summit, 2,280 feet above the sea and about 1,100 feet above the pond.

Returning, you'll find that some of the steeper pitches will challenge your snowplow and pole-dragging skills. Generally the trail is wide enough to keep you out of trouble, however, for it follows an old highway most of the way. Where you are skiing now, the farmers' wagons once toiled to the fields and pastures around Peaked Hill Pond.

23 Avalanche Camp

To clearing and return: 6 miles

Difficulty: slight

Map: AMC Franconia

Waterville Valley is a summer and winter resort entirely surrounded by the National Forest, with only 500 acres of privately owned land within its borders. It has a gorgeous network of hiking trails, the work of the Waterville Valley Athletic and Improvement Association, and many of these have been adapted for skiing. If you possibly can, obtain a copy of the "Goodrich map" published by the WVAIA and showing these trails with the ski routes marked in red. The maps ($1) are sometimes available at the Mobil station on the Mount Tecumseh access road, a left turn off NH 49 just before it enters the village.

The Livermore Logging Road is not part of the valley's ski-touring network, but the Touring Center is a convenient reference point nevertheless. It's a red building on your right at the very end of NH 49. To the left is West Branch Road: follow it ¾ mile to a junction, then turn right ¼ mile to Depot Clearing. Here the town has plowed a parking area exclusively for skiers.

The Livermore Logging Road goes straight ahead—past a gate, over a bridge, past the entrance to Greeley Ponds Trail, and over another bridge. This second bridge crosses the Mad River, a tributary of the Pemigewasset. There are fine views both upstream and

Wintry conditions add spice to backcountry touring, but skiers must prepare accordingly.

23 Avalanche Camp

down. Soon after, the road begins to climb uphill and to the left; on your right is a sign for Boulder Path. (A detour on this path is well worth the time, for it leads in 100 yards to a very large "erratic"—one of the mighty boulders scattered across New Hampshire by the glaciers—right in the middle of Slide Brook. *Caution:* the ice may be thin, especially where the water swirls around the boulder.) That first uphill climb is the steepest of the day, so don't lose heart. Regard it as a test of your waxing skill.

The forest along here is mixed hardwood and softwood, but it will soon give way to hardwoods exclusively, with only an occasional evergreen growing in their shade—a reminder of the logging activity that once denuded this entire area. At the turn of the century, Depot Clearing was the bustling headquarters for half a dozen cutting operations, and the Livermore Logging Road dates back to those boom times. It is now maintained by the Forest Service.

The road continues wide and handsome, passing Big Pines Trail and Kettles Trail on the left. Neither of these is suitable for skiing. About 1½ miles from the start, Slide Brook is visible on your right; the road and brook keep each other company for a time. A ski trail (experts only) crosses the brook and soon leads to Norway Rapids, but it was not passable when we went through.

About 2½ miles from Depot Clearing, the Loop Trail to South Tripyramid leaves on your right, and in another ½ mile you reach the small clearing that is your destination. This is the site of Avalanche Camp. It's not very impressive today, but it once housed a platoon of loggers plus their cooks, teamsters, and horses. In the summer you'd be able to search through the brambles for relics of

Avalanche Camp

these sturdy men, whose workday ran from half an hour before sunrise to half an hour after sunset—or twelve hours, whichever was less. Their spiked boots trampled the earth so thoroughly that, after the passage of nearly two generations, no tree yet grows on the battered ground.

From the clearing you can enjoy a vista for the first time since crossing Mad River: a rolling ridge to the north and east. Have your lunch here, if the wind isn't high. The road continues for another mile to the site of Flume Brook Camp, but it is decidedly steeper, narrower, and rougher than the route you have been following—recommended for advanced skiers only, especially on the descent. As it is, you may have occasion to practice your snowplow and pole-dragging techniques as you descend the 3 miles to Depot Clearing.

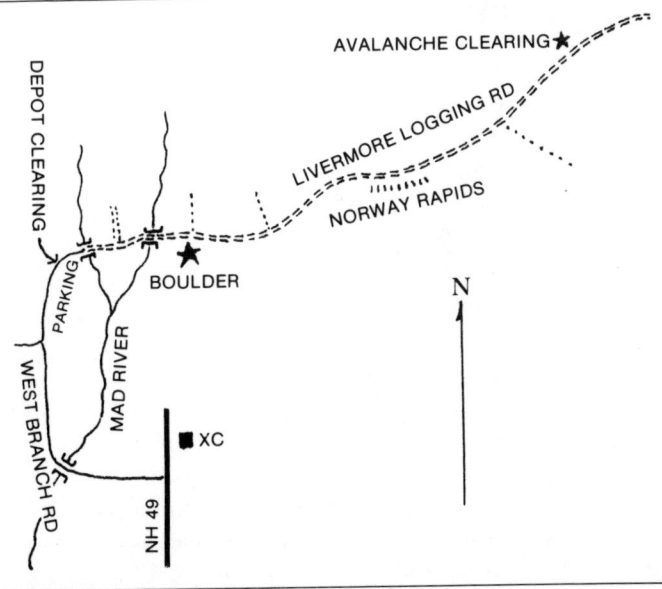

24 Greeley Ponds

To upper pond
and return:
7 miles

Difficulty:
moderate

Map: AMC
Franconia

We considered the Mad River Notch to be quite an expedition in 1971, when we first skied up to this picturesque cleft in the mountains above Waterville Valley. In those days it was actually possible to lose your way on Greeley Ponds Trail, a summer footpath which made no concessions to the winter traveler: it kept sending us from one bank of the Mad River to the other, and for a time it had us chasing along the frozen surface of the stream. Things have changed mightily in the past few years. More than 10,000 people register at the Waterville Valley Ski Touring Center in an average winter—an unimaginable increase over 1971. Not all of them are interested in backcountry touring, of course. Nevertheless, we knew that ski touring had become a mass recreation when we headed up the old trail and found ourselves greeted by this sign:

PLEASE KEEP TO THE RIGHT

The trail's popularity is well deserved. It's an easy grade almost to the height-of-land; the river crossings have been either bridged or bypassed; and the upper pond is as pretty as any you'll find in the White Mountains, tucked in a cleft between Mount Osceola and Mount Kancamagus.

24 Greeley Ponds

The trail actually begins on the Livermore Logging Road (see previous tour). Leave your car at Depot Clearing and ski across the Forest Service bridge onto the unplowed lumber road. In 100 yards, turn left onto Greeley Ponds Trail, which itself is a graded road for about one-third of its distance. You'll soon pick up Mad River—a rather subdued lunatic at this stage of its career—and will stay close to it for the rest of your journey. Scaur Trail leaves on the right and Goodrich Rock Trail on the left, neither of them suitable for skiing. About 1 mile from Depot Clearing, the trail crosses to the right bank on a

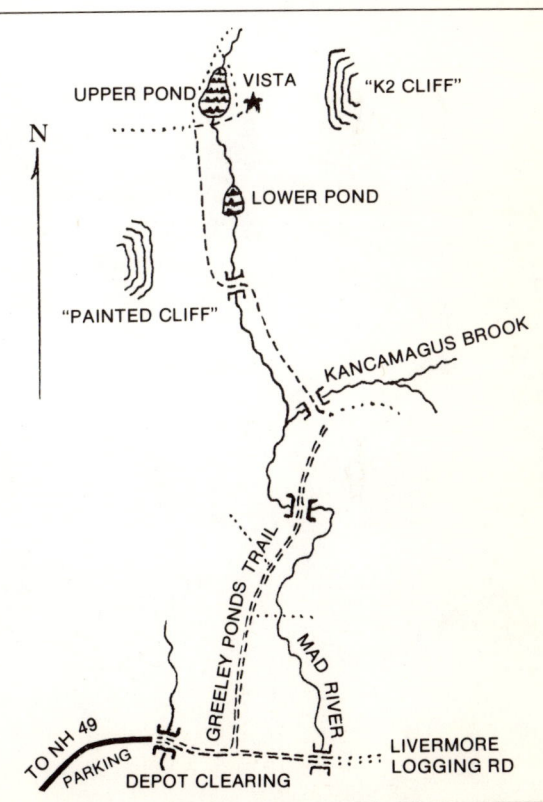

The Mad River plunges down toward Waterville Valley from its source in Greeley Ponds.

Greeley Ponds

footbridge. After passing a side-trail to the Flume, it crosses Kancamagus Brook on a recently constructed bridge of logs. (The Flume trail can be used as a link in a long and arduous tour to Kancamagus Basin, returning on the Livermore Logging Road.)

A dramatic knob of rock, known locally as "Painted Cliff," is visible on the left, keeping you company as you cross the boundary of the Greeley Ponds Scenic Area. This 810-acre preserve was established in 1964 to protect Mad River Notch from overuse. Almost directly beneath Painted Cliff, the trail returns to the left bank of Mad River. From here on, the terrain is somewhat steeper and decidedly more rugged. About 3 miles from Depot Clearing, the lower pond comes into view, rather bleak with dead trees projecting from its surface. The trail passes close to the shore and can be hard to follow if snow has covered the track— as it frequently does, for the wind blows hard through Mad River Notch.

In ½ mile the trail emerges at the foot of the upper pond, where Osceola Trail leaves on the left and a trail to the former wilderness shelter leaves on the right. Though the shelter was torn down several years ago as part of the effort to protect the area, the site still provides the best picnic spot in the vicinity. It commands a fine view of the pond, Painted Cliff, and the avalanche scars on Osceola East Peak; directly behind it is "K2 Cliff" on a spur of Mount Kancamagus. The spot is reached by skiing 100 yards to the east, across the outlet of the pond.

The height-of-land is ½ mile farther and can be reached either by returning to the west bank of the pond or by continuing along the spur trail on the east bank. Greeley Ponds Trail is skiable all the way to the Kancamagus Highway, only 1½ miles from the upper pond, but the

24 Greeley Ponds

road shuttle is so great that you'd have to ski back the way you came, unless you'd previously arranged to swap keys with another party of skiers.

On the return trip to Depot Clearing, beware of all stream crossings, and especially the first one. It's easy to pick up speed on the descent, and the new bridges were devilishly constructed at right angles to the trail.

25 Sandwich Notch Road

To "1776" and return: 11 miles

Difficulty: moderate

Map: AMC Chocorua-Waterville

The rough dirt road through Sandwich Notch provides one of the loveliest ski tours in the White Mountains, rich in history and almost totally unspoiled. (If you regard snowmobiles as spoilers, plan this trek for a weekday.) Incredibly, the road is privately owned for most of its length. At this writing there is a quiet campaign to add Sandwich Notch to the National Forest, and its present owner—a logging company—has agreed to leave the roadside untouched until its future is settled.

The best approach is from the south. Drive to Center Sandwich on NH 113 and take the Diamond Ledge Road northwest out of the village. Though paved for part of its length, this soon becomes a country lane with scarcely enough room for oncoming cars to pass each other; if you have tire chains, you would do well to put them on. About 2½ miles from the village, the Sandwich Notch Road forks to the left. It is unplowed and identified by a small sign nailed to a tree. The right fork bears a much larger sign for the Mead Wilderness Camp and is plowed wide enough for cars to be left at the intersection.

Ski along the unplowed road, which is level for a few hundred yards but which soon begins to climb. (On the

Sandwich Notch Road

Sandwich Notch Road, the uphills tend to leave you breathless from exertion while the downhills leave you breathless from excitement.) About 1 mile from the start, Bearcamp River loops around the road in an area known as Three Bridges; just above the first of these bridges, on the right, is the great boulder from which Joseph Meader preached to the farmers who lived in Sandwich Notch. They were a peculiar folk, and they preferred to worship at Pulpit Rock and its natural amphitheater, rather than go down to the meeting house in Sandwich.

Rolling up and down—but mostly up—the road follows the river for another mile to the high ground known as Mount Delight, marking the end of the Saco River watershed. Just beyond is a level stretch and a clearing

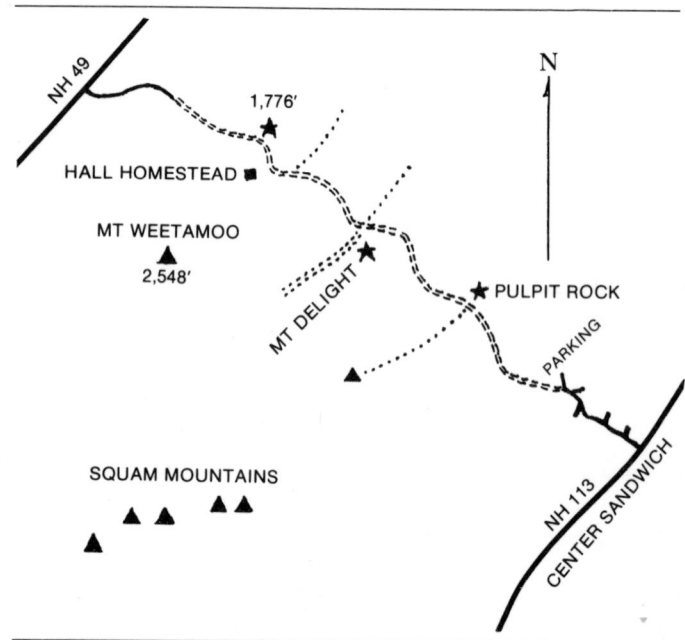

Sandwich Notch Road

of several acres—the only such clearing on the unplowed section of Sandwich Notch Road, which a century ago was entirely given over to farmyards, pasture, and orchard land. Northward you can see the Sandwich Ridge, with Mount Weetamoo as its dominant peak; southward lies the Squam Ridge.

The next stream you cross is the Beebe River, flowing west to join the Pemigewasset near Campton Hollow. There's a lumber road (not shown on the AMC map) which snowmobilers use to gain access to Sandwich Notch or to pass through to Guinea Pond on the east. This crossing is 3 miles from the beginning of Sandwich Notch Road, which now climbs steeply and passes beneath a power line (likewise missing from the map). The Algonquin Trail leaves on the right, then there's a bridge over the second head of Beebe River, and suddenly a small white house appears like a ghost on the left side of the road. This is the Hall homestead, the main structure built in 1877, but with a woodshed dating back to 1826. Moses Hall died in 1930, leaving $12,500 to the town for the maintenance of the Sandwich Notch Road. At that time, $12,500 probably would have sufficed to buy the entire length of the road for posterity.

After a steep uphill climb, the height-of-land is reached at 1,776 feet of altitude—not quite 900 vertical feet above your starting point, but considerably more than that if you count all the dips and rises you have skied in the past 5½ miles. From this point (marked by a hand-lettered sign) you will probably want to ski back the way you came. The road continues for 3 miles more, steeply downhill for the most part; its terminus on NH 49 would leave you about 40 miles from your automobile as the pavement runs.

Sandwich Notch Road

It's possible to ski the road one-way from Campton, at its northern end, by waiting for the end of March and the annual Sandwich Notch Open. This event began in 1975 for the purpose of raising money to save the notch; it attracts family tourers, flat-out racing types, and even a few dozen snowshoers. The entry fee at this writing was $5, including soft drinks halfway, cocoa and a hot fire at the finish, and bus transportation back to your starting point in Campton. For information, contact the Ski Touring Center, Waterville Valley NH 03223.

Several hundred skiers, young and old, compete each year in the Sandwich Notch Open.

25 Tips from 25 Tours

1. Backpacks. We never leave home without our packs, even for a two-mile ski to the local beaver dam. We carry spare clothing—even to down parka and mittens—and such emergency gear as a first-aid kit, flashlight, compass, can of Sterno, aluminized rescue blanket, spare ski tip, jackknife, matches, and whistle. Choosing a pack and filling it are highly personal matters. A waistband is essential for skiing, to keep the pack from jumping about; a frame and padded shoulder straps are advisable if you'll regularly be carrying more than 10 pounds. Once you've found the right combination, keep it packed and ready to go. Then you won't leave anything vital at home.

2. Hats. "If your feet are cold, put on a hat"—so goes the wisdom of the backcountry. With your head uncovered at 40°, about half your heat loss is through the scalp. A hat is therefore a splendid thermostat for skiers: clap it on if you're chilly, pull it off when you're warm. The most useful design is the Balaclava helmet, costing about $6 at mountain specialty stores, which serves at will as hat, neck warmer, and even face mask.

3. Glove liners. They come in silk or an aluminized fabric, and they don't add much in the way of warmth. But they're a blessing when you must take off your mittens to eat lunch, operate a camera, or tinker with straps and strings.

4. Down vests. The fashionable way to wear a vest is on top of a windshirt, which is pretty but not very efficient. Rather, the windbreaker—not a windshirt, either, but a nylon or cotton-nylon shell with a drawstring waist and hood—should be sized

Tips

to fit over the vest. The combination rivals a parka for warmth. Touring with the vest open, you might as well be skiing in your shirtsleeves; when you stop for a moment, you simply zip up the vest for added warmth. And for a lunch break or a turn in the weather, the windbreaker goes over all. Incidentally, a vest need not be filled with "prime northern goosedown" to do an effective job. Duck down is perfectly good, and down substitutes such as PolarGuard and Fiberfill II have the advantage of providing warmth even when wet.

5. Wool. This is winter! These are the White Mountains of New Hampshire! If vanity compels you to ski in a racing costume, with low-cut shoes and ventilated gloves, carry extra clothing to go under or over them. Of all fabrics, wool is still the most desirable for winter travelers. Wool socks, wool mittens, wool hat or Balaclava, wool shirt and sweater, and especially wool or wool-blend underwear—they'll keep you warm, blow wet, blow dry.

6. Fishnet. If you can't bear to have wool next to the skin, try the Norwegian fishnet underwear. Its thermal qualities are legendary—perhaps mythical. However that may be, the fishnet has the tremendous virtue of feeling dry even when it isn't.

7. Staying dry. Water at 50° is unbearably cold. This is true whether you fall into a stream, get caught in a rainstorm, or allow yourself to become soaked with sweat. Skiers who travel hard sometimes carry a quaint item of survival gear—a dry undershirt! Better yet, don't work up a sweat in the first place. Have nylon shell clothing—windpants as well as a windbreaker—to shed the snow. Carry a poncho or a waterproof jacket if there's a chance of rain.

8. Tea. Exercise in the winter involves breathing air that is cold and dry, then exhaling it warm and moist. You also lose a lot of water through insensible sweat. The most pleasant way to make good the loss is to drink hot tea, preferably weak (so you'll drink more of it) and sweet (to provide a bit of energy as well). If carrying a thermos bottle goes against the grain, try insulat-

Tips

ing a canteen with a pair of wool socks, which are useful extras in their own right.

9. Gorp. Every serious wilderness traveler has a recipe for "gorp"—trail food high in energy, low in weight, and easy to eat. For day trips you needn't be fancy. Just mix raisins, peanuts, and chocolate drops in equal proportions . . . put a cupful in a plastic sandwich bag . . . give one baggie to each member of the party . . . and you can ski from sunup to sundown without suffering hunger pangs. Going the gorp route also ensures that you won't litter the trail with orange peels and candybar wrappers.

10. Sitting. A picnic lunch is one of the nicest rituals of skiing, but where to sit? Skis and packs make uncomfortable seats, especially if the skis are waxed with klister and the pack contains your dessert. A poncho is dry but chilly. Warmup pants are better, if the snow isn't too wet, and best of all is a combination of the two. Don't begrudge the weight, for each is worth carrying as emergency gear. If you like to specialize, buy an ensolite pad of the type used by winter campers to put under their sleeping bags.

11. Kids. Leave small children at home, for they don't possess the stamina for backcountry touring, nor are they especially interested in it. At eight or nine—maybe. (Skiing with Kate, we found that she'd handle a difficult trail with more grace than a lengthy one.) Kids have a tendency to plop down in the snow, to drop their mittens, and to keep going until they melt; the wisest precaution is not to take them skiing in very cold weather. Insulated workboots are warmer than ski-touring boots, and cheaper as well. Children's skis should be short— head height, nose height, even chin height for the very young. Chocolate bars will keep the youngsters moving when threats or pleading are of no avail. Of the tours in this book, we've child-tested the Flume, the Old Man of the Mountains (one way), and Diana's Baths. They're not only short, but each has a fascinating object along the way.

At times like this, a skier is apt to think more kindly of skis that require no waxing.

Tips

12. Waxing. In the hard waxes, Bratlie blue and Swix purple are easy to apply outdoors and have an extremely wide range between them. (Thin out the blue for cold weather; let the purple go gooey when things begin to melt.) In the klisters, Swix purple has the same virtues. We have no advice on the matter of blue klister (difficult to apply) and red klister (prone to leak out of its container).

13. No-waxing. Waxless skis are ideal for children and beginners. They're also suited for the backcountry, where you don't have a warm room and a blowtorch to help you change from one wax to another. Yes, a good skier can go faster on the traditional bases, but he'll go a considerable distance before making up for the time spent in waxing them.

14. Bindings. Except in children's sizes, most stores don't even sell the sturdy old cable binding any longer. You'll almost certainly do your touring in a toe-clamp binding that was adapted from racing gear. Take the time to understand its workings. Carry an extra bail (the part that bears upon your shoe) in case this vital element flies off into the snow. Carry a screwdriver and a length of cord; if the binding should break, you can loosen the screws and slip the cord beneath what remains of the metal plate, then tighten the screws again and fashion a toe-strap or heel harness as the case demands.

15. Poles. Ski-touring books often begin with an illustration of how to put your hand through the strap of your ski-pole. Don't!—not when skiing through trees or undergrowth where you might snag the basket. True, if you drop a pole you'll be obliged to return for it, but that's a whole lot easier than returning for your arm. If you are determined to use the straps for backcountry touring, then equip your poles with breakaway straps of the sort gaining favor with downhill skiers.

16. Snowplowing. The snowplow is a necessary part of touring technique, but it does have a tendency to lead to crossed tips, locked knees, and other hazardous postures. Much more satisfactory—especially when the snow is glassy-surfaced or

Tips

very heavy—is *half* a snowplow. Let one ski do the braking while the other runs straight and controls the direction of travel. You'll find that you can stay looser in the joints, that you can control your speed by putting more or less weight on the braking ski, and that you can avoid fatigue by braking first with one ski and then with the other.

17. Where are you? Carry a trail map and compass whenever you ski the backcountry, and know how to use them. (The cheapest Silva compass costs $5, is perfectly adequate, and comes with useful instruction booklet.) You should also leave your itinerary with someone—parent, innkeeper, friend—who will take action if you don't return in good time. At the very least, leave a note on the windshield of your car.

18. Maps. The easiest way to obtain a set of trail maps is to buy the *AMC White Mountain Guide,* available for $8 at any good New England bookstore. The individual maps are sold for 50¢ or $1 at mountain specialty shops, but to go into the backcountry without the *AMC Guide* is as foolish as to go without your mittens. A useful supplement in the Eastern Slope region is the Jackson Ski Touring Map, available locally for $1. You can manage with the appropriate AMC sheet and careful attention to trail signs, but it's all laid out for you in red on the Jackson sheet. Personally, we found the USGS quadrangles a mixed blessing. They're splendid for visualizing the countryside, but their roads and trails are often out of date and sometimes inaccurately shown. The USGS sheets are usually available at hardware stores, mountain speciality shops, and bookstores in the White Mountain region.

19. Survival gear. The Tacoma Mountain Rescue Unit sells a "Storm Kit" which includes a one-person tube tent, matches, candle, whistle, bouillion cubes, teabags, and sugar. It comes in a waterproof container the size of a tobacco tin; the lid can be used as a mirror for signaling, and with a wire bail (also provided) the container serves as a cup. The whole thing weighs 11 ounces and costs $3 postpaid. Address: PO Box 696, Tacoma WA 98401.

Tips

20. Pockets. Nothing is more frustrating than to search with cold fingers for the compass—or the map—or a bite to eat. Experience will soon tell you which items you need most often; you should then distribute these in the pockets of your trousers, shirt or windbreaker, and the pack itself according to a system that never changes. In a phrase: a pocket for everything, and everything in its pocket.

21. Straps. When all else fails and you decide to walk home, one or two straps to hold your skis together will make carrying them infinitely less unpleasant, especially if their bases are smeared with klister.

22. Trees. Half the joy of touring is to discover new things about yourself and your world. One delightful avenue for exploration is the forest itself—to learn that certain beech and oak retain their leaves in winter, that spruce is prickly while fir is soft, that you can identify the local species of pine by counting the needles in a cluster. . . . All this and more from a pocket-sized book called *Trees and Shrubs of Northern New England,* published by the Society for the Protection of New Hampshire Forests and available for $2.50 in most bookstores.

23. Kilometers. Many touring centers have gone metric, while hiking trails are still measured in miles. We decided to be traditional. If you find yourself on a metric trail and want to know the distance in miles, you must multiply by 5 and divide by 8. Reverse the procedure if you want to convert miles to kilometers. Here's a table in case you'd rather not bother:

Kilometers:	1	1.6	4	6.4	**8**	10	12.8	18
Miles:		⅝	1	2½	4	**5**	6¼	8	11¼

24. Being stuck. It's bound to happen sooner or later, if you persist in driving the back roads in winter. A shovel and a container of sand are therefore essential, and tire chains are not entirely out of place. Put some salt in the sand to keep it from freezing. A milk carton makes a convenient container and serves as an emergency flare when empty.

Tips

25. Snowmobiles. Someday the snowmobilers will get smart and buy cross-country skis. Until that happy day, you can avoid them almost entirely by staying away from snowmobile corridors on weekends and holidays. About half the tours in this book are open to snowmobiles. Yet we met the infernal machines only twice—and each time was a Saturday. Otherwise we saw only their tracks, which proved to be a help as often as they proved to be a hindrance.